how to

Teach
Writing

Longman

Jeremy
Harmer

Pearson Education Limited
Edinburgh Gate
Harlow
Essex
CM20 2JE
England
and Associated Companies throughout the world.

www.longman.com

Printed in Malaysia
Second impression 2004

Produced for the publishers by Stenton Associates, Saffron Walden, Essex, UK. Text design by Keith Rigley. Illustrations by Ian Evans and Jackie Harland.

ISBN 0582 77998 7

Acknowledgements

We are grateful to the following for permission to reproduce copyright material:

Five Islands Press for an extract from 'Welcome' by Cate Kennedy published in *Signs of Other Fires*; Guardian Newspapers Limited for extracts adapted from 'Grandparents juggle career and caring' by John Carvel published in *The Guardian* 2 October 2002 © The Guardian 2002, 'Big Freeze Brings Travel Chaos' published in *The Guardian* 31 January 2003 © The Guardian 2003, and 'Respiro' by Philip French published in *The Observer* 10 September 2003 © The Observer 2003; Marshall Cavendish Limited for extracts adapted from *Just Right Upper Intermediate* by Jeremy Harmer © Marshall Cavendish Limited 2004, and an extract adapted from *Just Reading and Writing* by Jeremy Harmer © Marshall Cavendish Limited 2004; the author's agent for the poem 'In Two Minds' by Roger McGough published in *Everyday Eclipses* © 2003, Roger McGough; Modern English Publishing for extracts adapted from 'The newspaper project: Working together to make a class newspaper' by Victoria Chan published in *Modern English Teacher* 10/1 (2001), and 'Introducing the narrative essay: a painless way to start an academic writing programme' by Linda Pearce published in *Modern English Teacher* 7/1 (1998); Oxford University Press for extracts from *Writing* by Tricia Hedge © Oxford University Press 1988, *English File Upper Intermediate Student's Book* by Clive Oxenden and Christina Latham-Koenig © Oxford University Press 2001, and *New Headway English Course Intermediate Student's Book* by Liz and John Soars © Oxford University Press 1996; St Matthew's Primary School, Cambridge for the poem 'To Philip' by Tanya published in *Poets Live in Cambridge Anthology* edited by H. Cook and Y. Bradbury; Thames Valley Police for a sample letter of theirs; and W.W. Norton & Company for the poem 'It May Not Always Be So' by E.E. Cummings published in *Complete Poems 1904–1962* edited by George J. Firmage © 1991 by the Trustees for the E.E. Cummings Trust and George James Firmage.

In some instances we have been unable to trace the owners of copyright material and we would appreciate any information that would enable us to do so.

The Publishers are grateful to the following for their permission to reproduce copyright photographs:

The British Library for page 2; Andrew Cooney for page 56 top; Mark Anthony Franklin/R3MAF for page 141 left and right; Harrapa.com for page 1; Kingfisher plc for 56 bottom; National Portrait Gallery, London for page 68 left and right; PA Photos for page 95; Punchstock/Image 100 for pages 26 and 27

Contents

Introduction

Who is this book for?

How to Teach Writing has been written for teachers of English who are interested in writing as a process and in the variety of types of writing, and who would like to use their understanding of these ideas in the activities they offer their students.

What is this book about?

For as long as languages have been taught, teachers have asked students to write things in their notebooks and exercise books. Yet sometimes, over the years, it has seemed that writing has been seen as only a support system for learning grammar and vocabulary, rather than as a skill in its own right. Recently, however, trainers and methodologists have looked again at writing in the foreign-language classroom and put forward ways of teaching this skill which acknowledge and emphasise its importance. Anyone who doubts this only needs to look at the list of significant books on the subject on page 149.

How to Teach Writing starts by looking at the process that a competent speaker of English goes through after they decide to write a piece of text, and at how our understanding of this has implications for the way we should approach the teaching of writing. The second chapter is a discussion of various types of writing, or genres, and of the role of genre study in teaching writing. Chapter 3 suggests that a mix of process and genre work can be offered in writing activities, and shows how this can be done. Chapter 4 looks at some of the nuts and bolts of writing (including handwriting, spelling, and punctuation) before going on to show examples of activities designed to help students write coherently in sentences and paragraphs.

One of the obstacles that writing teachers have to overcome, at times, is a reluctance on the part of their students to engage in writing activities with any enthusiasm. Chapter 5 addresses this problem by describing activities designed specifically to build the writing habit – activities which should enthuse student writers, build their confidence, and make them feel comfortable with writing.

In Chapter 6, we draw together much of what has been said about process and genre with a look at more 'worked-on' writing – writing which students have time to think about, plan, and edit. In Chapter 7, the way teachers react to students' writing is considered. Should we correct with red ink, or respond with comments and suggestions? It is clear that the way we deal with students' writing can have a profound effect on how they feel about writing.

Chapter 8 looks at journal writing as a tool for reflection and as a way of promoting written fluency; it is also a way that teachers and students can enter into a new kind of dialogue.

Suggested classroom activities are signalled by this icon .

Finally, a Task File allows the reader to review and develop some of the ideas dealt with here. An answer key is provided. This is followed by two appendices: the first gives a brief summary of punctuation rules, and the second offers chapter notes and further reading suggestions.

Acknowledgements

This book would have been impossible without the inspired writing of theorists, methodologists, and teachers such as Donn Byrne, William Grabe and Robert Kaplan, Ken Hyland, Tricia Hedge, Chris Tribble, Ron White and Valerie Arndt. Anyone who wishes to talk about writing feels a deep sense of gratitude for their insights and wisdom.

Closer to home, I would like to express my thanks to the Taiwanese teachers I worked with at the Bell School of Languages in Cambridge, UK, as well as my students at Anglia Polytechnic University here in the same city. Because I was especially interested in putting this book together, their writings – and responses to written activities – were always interesting and challenging.

As this book has developed, I have benefited enormously from the intelligent comment and creative criticisms of David A Hill, whose skill and suggestions have been invaluable. And, as usual, all this starts and ends with David Lott, a publisher and editor like no other, without whom writing about teaching and learning would, for me, be less interesting, less eye-opening, and less worthwhile. Thanks are hardly enough.

Anyway, I do thank all these people. But I'm responsible for what you are going to read, not them. I have just been lucky enough to lean on their knowledge, skills, and input.

Writing as a process

This writing business, pencils and what not, overrated if you ask me.
Eeyore in 'Winnie the Pooh' by A A Milne

- **From the beginning**
- **Why learn to write?**
- **How people write**
- **Writing and speaking**
- **Implications for learning and teaching**

From the beginning

If mankind, in the form of *Homo sapiens*, can be traced back to 100,000 years ago, then the human activity of writing is a fairly recent development in the evolution of men and women. Some of the earliest writing found so far dates from about 5,500 years ago. It was found in 1999 at a place called Harappa in the region where the great Harappan or Indus civilisation once flourished. There is incomplete agreement about the meaning of the symbols that were discovered. However, when the discovery was made, the archaeologist Richard Meadow stated that the inscriptions had similarities to what became the Indus script – the first recognised written language:

Symbols on Harappan pottery

Since then, many different writing systems have evolved around the world. For example, the following multilingual offers (for translation into the reader's language) give a flavour of some of them:

Osoby ktore by chcialy azeby ten list byl przet umaczony na jezyk Polski so proszone o zaznaczenie kwadratu na prawo. Prosze odeslac list, razem z ta kartka pod adres <u>44 St Andrews Street, Cambridge</u>. Postaramy sie przeslac tresc listu w przetlumaczeniu na jezyk Polski w przeciagu siedmiu dni.

Bu mektubun Türkçeye tercüme edilmesini isterseniz, lütfen sağdaki kutuyu işaretleyiniz. Mektubu ve bu sayfayı 44 St. Andrews Street Cambridge adresimize gönderiniz; yedi gün içinde mektubu size Türkçe olarak göndereceğiz.

Nếu quí khách muốn lá thơ này được dịch sang tiếng Việt, xin vui lòng gạch vào ô bên tay phải dưới đây. Xin gởi lá thơ và tờ giấy này đến: <u>44 St Andrews Street, Cambridge</u>, và chúng tôi sẽ gởi cho quí khách một bản bằng tiếng Việt trong vòng 7 ngày.

如果你想此信翻譯成中文，請於右面方格上劃上一剔，連同此信及附頁寄回 44 St Andrews Street, Cambridge，中文譯本將會於七天內寄給你。

જો તમે આ પત્રનું ગુજરાતી ભાષામાં ભાષાંતર કરવામાં આવે તેવું ઇચ્છતા હો તો જમણી બાજુનાં બોકસમાં નિશાન કરો. આ પત્ર અને આ પાનુ અમને 44 St. Andrews Street, Cambridge, એ સરનામે પરત મોકલો અને અમે તમને સાત દિવસની અંદરોઅંદર ગુજરાતી ભાષામાં એક નકલ મોકલી આપીશું.

Some of the many translation offers for/in different languages, Cambridge City Council, UK

English writing has changed considerably over the centuries. Early fourteenth-century writing, for example, had significantly different spellings from present-day English and some letters were formed differently too:

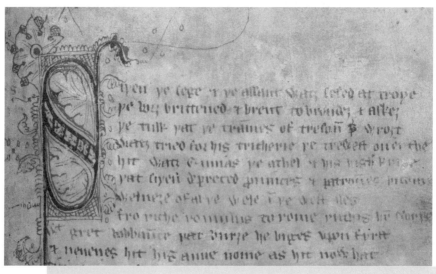

An extract from *Sir Gawain and the Green Knight*, written in the fourteenth century

A modern version of written (or 'texted') communication, however, received via a mobile phone, can look like this message. Clearly 'writing' has come a long way – or, has it?!

Why learn to write?

However long ago writing really started, it has remained for most of its history a minority occupation. This is in part because although almost all human beings grow up speaking their first language (and sometimes their second or third) as a matter of course, writing has to be taught. Spoken language, for a child, is acquired naturally as a result of being exposed to it, whereas the ability to write has to be consciously learned.

It is only in the last two hundred years or so that **literacy** – that is being able to read and write – has been seen as a desirable skill for whole populations. Before that it was most likely to be used by rulers of church and state only. Too much knowledge was not thought to be a good thing for the majority of the working population. But as societies grew larger and more industrialised, the need for citizens to be able to write and read became vital in order for bureaucratic organisation to be successful. And then it became clear that education (including **numeracy** – as well as literacy) was desirable for the whole population, not just for the efficient running of society, but also for the fulfilment and advancement of individuals. Thus we no longer have to ask ourselves whether writing is a good thing or not. We take it as a fundamental right. As Chris Tribble says in his book on writing, 'to be deprived of the opportunity to learn to write is … to be excluded from a wide range of social roles, including those which the majority of people in industrialised societies associate with power and prestige'.

But all over the world people are deprived of precisely that right. According to the Canadian organisation WLC (World Literacy Canada), there are at least 875 million illiterate adults in the world, of whom two thirds are women and there are at least a hundred million children worldwide (60 million of them girls) who still have no access to primary education.

Yet education transforms lives and societies and the ability to read, and write, and being numerate gives adults and children a huge advantage over those who are not so fortunate.

In the context of education, it is also worth remembering that most exams, whether they are testing foreign language abilities or other skills, often rely on the students' writing proficiency in order to measure their knowledge.

Eeyore the donkey, whose quote started this chapter, is wrong to say that writing is a waste of time, therefore, even if he does sound like every sulky student who has ever complained! Being able to write is a vital skill for 'speakers' of a foreign language as much as for everyone using their own first

How people write

language. Training students to write thus demands the care and attention of language teachers.

Because writing is used for a wide variety of purposes it is produced in many different forms. The shopping list below, for example, written over a couple of days as shortages in the kitchen were noticed, is a type of writing that many people (who might not think of themselves as 'writers') do, as a matter of course. A number of features of this list are of interest to us when we consider how people write. In the first place, the writer clearly has an audience in mind for their writing (themselves). In the second place, the writer has clearly changed their mind on more than one occasion, both deleting and adding items on the list. However, this editing of the list has only gone so far: in their haste they have misspelt a word (a brand name) and have not corrected it, seeing no reason to check through their writing (for accuracy). Lastly, it is worth noting the use of a foreign word (*cilantro*), obviously known to the writer. This word would probably not have been used if the list had been written for a general English-speaking audience.

> Chutney
> Tobacco
> Toothpaste
> Chicken
> Rice
> Cilantro
> Real peas
> Crackers
> Ice cream biscuits
> Necaff

Although this shopping list may not seem to provide an example of sophisticated writing, it nevertheless tells us something about the writing **process** – that is the stages a writer goes through in order to produce something in its final written form. This process may, of course, be affected by the **content** (subject matter) of the writing, the type of writing (shopping lists, letters, essays, reports, or novels), and the **medium** it is written in (pen and paper, computer word files, live chat, etc.). But in all of these cases it is suggested that the process has four main elements:

Planning

Experienced writers plan what they are going to write. Before starting to write or type, they try and decide what it is they are going to say. For some writers this may involve making detailed notes. For others a few jotted words may be enough. Still others may not actually write down any preliminary notes at all since they may do all their planning in their heads. But they will have planned, nevertheless, just as the shopping list writer has thought – at some level of consciousness – about what food is needed before writing it on the piece of paper.

When planning, writers have to think about three main issues. In the first place they have to consider the **purpose** of their writing since this will influence (amongst other things) not only the type of text they wish to produce, but also the language they use, and the information they choose to include. Secondly, experienced writers think of the **audience** they are writing for, since this will influence not only the shape of the writing (how it is laid out, how the paragraphs are structured, etc.), but also the choice of language – whether, for example, it is formal or informal in tone. Thirdly, writers have to consider the **content structure** of the piece – that is, how best to sequence the facts, ideas, or arguments which they have decided to include.

Drafting

We can refer to the first version of a piece of writing as a **draft**. This first 'go' at a text is often done on the assumption that it will be amended later. As the writing process proceeds into editing, a number of drafts may be produced on the way to the final version.

Editing (reflecting and revising)

Once writers have produced a draft they then, usually, read through what they have written to see where it works and where it doesn't. Perhaps the order of the information is not clear. Perhaps the way something is written is ambiguous or confusing. They may then move paragraphs around or write a new introduction. They may use a different form of words for a particular sentence. More skilled writers tend to look at issues of general meaning and overall structure before concentrating on detailed features such as individual words and grammatical accuracy. The latter two are, of course, important and are often dealt with later in the process.

Reflecting and revising are often helped by other readers (or editors) who comment and make suggestions. Another reader's reaction to a piece of writing will help the author to make appropriate revisions.

Final version

Once writers have edited their draft, making the changes they consider to be necessary, they produce their final version. This may look considerably different from both the original plan and the first draft, because things have changed in the editing process. But the writer is now ready to send the written text to its intended audience.

We might decide to represent these stages in the following way:

Process 4 elements: **planning ➡ drafting ➡ editing ➡ final draft**

However, there are two reasons why this diagram is not entirely satisfactory. In the first place, it tells us little about how much weight is given to each stage, but, more importantly, by suggesting that the process of writing is linear it misrepresents the way in which the majority of writers produce written text. The process of writing is not linear, as indicated above, but rather **recursive**. This means that writers plan, draft, and edit but then often re-plan, **re**-draft, and **re**-edit. Even when they get to what they think is their final draft they may find themselves changing their mind and re-planning, drafting, or editing. They may even start – as some novelists do – without too much of a plan, and so their point of entry into the process is that first draft, a kind of 'stream of consciousness', that only later through a series of re-plannings, editings, and draftings gradually coalesces into a final version of the text.

We need to represent these aspects of the writing process in a different way, therefore; the **process wheel** below clearly shows the many directions that writers can take, either travelling backwards and forwards around the rim or going up and down the wheel's spokes. Only when the final version really <u>is</u> the final version has the process reached its culmination.

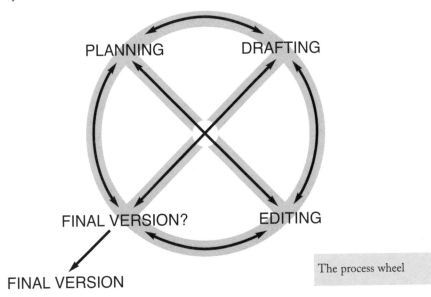

The process wheel

The writing process we have described operates whether people are writing e-mails, texting their friends, writing shopping lists, providing compositions for their English teachers, or putting together a doctoral thesis. How much attention we give to the different stages of the process (and to recursion in the process) will largely depend, as we have seen, on what kind of writing we are doing, what medium we are using, what the content and length of our piece is, and who we are doing it for. Sometimes the first three stages of the process will take almost no time at all and we will plan, (re-)draft, and (re-)edit very quickly in our heads as we write. Nevertheless, however casually we approach the process, we will still try and plan what to write, check what we have written, and revise it before sending it off. It is just that at certain times we do this more carefully than at others.

Writing and speaking

When considering how people write, we need to consider the similarities and differences between writing and speaking, both in terms of their forms and in the processes that writers and speakers go through to produce language. Despite the fact that the differences between the two forms are often very marked, there are also occasions when speaking and writing look very much the same – and are done in much the same way.

Time and space

Whereas spoken communication operates in the here-and-now world of immediate interaction, writing transcends time and space. Speaking is often transient, whereas writing tends to be more permanent. Spoken words fly away on the wind; written words stay around, sometimes, as we have seen, for hundreds or thousands of years.

Yet this essential difference between speaking and writing is not absolute. Text-messaging, for example, shares some of the same qualities of immediacy and transience (especially since messages are often erased the moment they have been read). Although people use the written word on the Internet, live sessions are not called *chats* by accident since when computer users are 'talking' to each other in real time, what they type looks more like speech than written discourse.

Some speech feels a lot like writing, too. Lectures, for example, are obviously spoken events, yet they are often read out from written notes or a complete text, and whether they are reconstituted from the lecturer's script or from the notes made by members of the audience, they have a permanence which more spontaneous spoken events lack.

Participants

A lot of spoken communication takes place between people who can see each other. Sometimes (as in the case of family members, friends, and close colleagues) we know each other well. On other occasions, where we are talking with relative strangers, we make assumptions about who we are talking to. In both cases we choose our words (with more or less care) on the basis of who these **co-participants** are. But even when we cannot see them (such as when we talk on the telephone), we still use our knowledge (in the case of people we know) or make assumptions (in the case of strangers) about who we are addressing, and this helps us to decide what to say and how to say it.

We have seen the importance of audience in the writing process, suggesting that one of an experienced writer's skills is the ability to know who they are writing for. However, this audience may often be general rather than specific, and may be represented as a type (a bank manager, a university admissions tutor, a possible business partner) rather than as an individual **addressee** who we can see and interact with. In the case of speaking, however, our addressee is often known to us in a much more specific way, as we have seen.

We can go further. When we are engaged in spoken communication we often decide what to say, as the conversation continues, on the basis of what our co-participants are saying. They may ask us for clarification or we may ask them. We may modify what we say on the basis of their verbal or non-verbal reactions. Instead of being able to get our points across unhindered, we may be constantly interrupted, and so have to proceed in a less structured way than we had anticipated. Furthermore, a unique feature of face-to-face communication is that addresser and addressee frequently swap roles as the conversation continues.

As with the issue of time and space, however, there are no clear-cut boundaries between speaking and writing. Sometimes a speaker is talking to a large number of people (at a meeting or in a lecture theatre) who are only co-participants in the broadest sense. Though their collective expression may help the speaker modify what he or she is saying, there is far less of the interaction we have been describing in smaller face-to-face encounters. As a writer, a poet or journalist, for example, may address him or herself to everyone and anyone, but a text message (such as the one on page 3) is much more like speaking in that the 'text messager' knew exactly who she was 'writing' to. In Internet chat rooms or live forums, addressers and addressees swap roles more like speakers than writers do.

Process

One of the most obvious differences between writing and speaking has to do with the processes that writers and speakers go through. In face-to-face communication there is little, if any, time lag between production and reception. Thought becomes word with great speed, and is absorbed as it appears. Once something is said it cannot be unsaid (though speakers can of course go back and say things differently in an attempt to modify the listener's understanding of what they are saying).

Because speech of this kind is so instant, speakers make quick decisions about what to say and modify it as they speak, using lots of repetition, rephrasing, and 'time-buying' expressions (such as *well, you know*). These expressions allow them to collect their ideas and put them into a suitable form of words. Writing, however, is, as we have seen, significantly different. The final product is not nearly so instant, and as a result the writer has a chance to plan and modify what will finally appear as the finished product. We have called this the writing process, with its recursiveness and multiple drafting.

Yet not all writing is as involved as this. There are no 'crossings-out' or visible changes in many postcards, though some planning may have gone into them. This is partly because postcard language and form is so predictable that constructing a text within it is relatively easy. Much Internet writing and text messaging could hardly be said to demonstrate a detailed process of the kind we have described. Speaking is not always a process-free act either. Careful speakers involve themselves in planning and drafting in their heads before they start to speak or before a pre-arranged conversational encounter (such as an interview, a meeting, or a difficult phone call) takes place. We may even rehearse what we are going to say. We often 'rewrite' conversations in our head after they have taken place, too. We tell ourselves that we wish we had thought of something wittier, cleverer, or more devastating than the words we actually used. The process of writing is usually more complex than the process of speaking, but not always.

Organisation and language

The way spontaneous speech and written text are constructed shows significant differences both in terms of organisation and the language used. A lot of writing follows a defined discourse organisation; typical English paragraph construction, for example, has a topic sentence followed by exemplification, then perhaps exceptions or further exemplification, and then a resolution or conclusion. Some conversations, it is true, follow pre-set patterns too. **Phatic** events, for example, are those where people have completely predictable exchanges such as:

A: How are you?
B: Fine. And you?
A: Fine.

The object here is not to convey real meaning but to maintain social harmony. However, many spoken exchanges are not nearly so easily predictable.

Two of the most noticeable dissimilarities between speaking and writing are the level of correctness and the issue of **well-formedness**. Speakers can and do mispronounce and use deviant grammar without anyone objecting or judging the speaker's level of intelligence and education, but spelling mistakes and grammar 'awkwardnesses', for example, are far more harshly judged. As for well-formedness, most writing consists of fully developed sentences, but speech is often made up of smaller chunks of language – words and phrases rather than complete sentences. A typical example of this is the use of **condensed questions**. In speech we often say single words like *Biscuit?* on their own to perform the whole question-asking function (*Would you like a biscuit?*). Unless we are writing an approximation of speech, this would of course be largely unacceptable in writing.

Another significant difference between speaking and writing concerns **lexical density** – that is the proportion of **content words** to **grammatical** (or **function**) **words** used. We are using a content word here to mean nouns, main verbs, adjectives, and most adverbs, which are all content-carrying words such as *flowers, run, orange, happily*. When we compare these to grammatical words, such as *if, was, and*, and *with* (which, of course, link the content words to make sentences), we find that written text frequently has many more content words than grammatical words. In speech, however, the proportion of content words is significantly smaller.

It is not just the higher proportion of content words that is a feature of writing; it is also the actual words used. The words *guy* and *cool* are very frequent in contemporary English speech, but not in writing, whereas *evidence* and *customary* are much more likely to occur in writing than in speaking. The verbs *let* and *allow* (which have similar meanings) are interesting in this respect; whereas *let* is much more common in speech than in writing, the reverse is the case for *allow*.

Certain lexical types are significantly less common in writing than in speech. Phrasal verbs (*take off, put up with, look after*, etc.) are much more likely to occur in conversation than in writing. We may also use hesitation markers (*umm, well*, etc.), non-clausal units (such as *Mmm, Uh huh*), and interjections (*Wow! Cor!* etc.) when we are speaking, in a way that we do not when producing written text. We use nonsense words (*thingamajig, whatd'youcallit*) in speech but not in writing.

Similarly, certain grammatical features are less common in writing than in speech, such as contracted verb forms (*isn't, won't,* etc.), tag questions (e.g. *You're English, aren't you?*), and echo questions (A: *I'm really unhappy.* B: *You're really unhappy?*).

Once again, however, we need to qualify this view of the differences between written and spoken language. Many of the conversational features we have mentioned are far less common when speech becomes more writing-like (as in a lecture, funeral oration, or political address). Spoken language features appear when writing aims to imitate speech (as in dialogue passages of a novel, or in a play), and a lot of modern electronic writing looks much more like conversation than prose. Indeed by obeying the principle of 'the fewer keystrokes the better', electronic communication has started to change some forms of writing by using numbers and single letters to approximate fuller written text (e.g. *CUL8R* for *See you later*).

Signs and symbols

Both writing and speaking have their own signs, symbols, and devices to make communication more effective. In face-to-face conversations speakers and listeners use expression and gesture, as well as stress and intonation, to convey meaning. We can vary the tone or speed of what we are saying, or fill our conversation with dramatic pauses if we want to. We can shout or we can whisper. These elements – body language and the ways we use our voices – are called **paralinguistic features**; they are not language as such but are used in parallel with language.

Writing has fewer signs and symbols than speech but they can be just as powerful. In the first place, question marks and exclamation marks can modify the import of what is written (e.g. *You are cold. You are cold? You are cold!* or even *You are cold!!!*). By changing the order of clauses we can alter meaning and convey nuance (e.g. *She met him at a party.* or *At a party she met him.* or *Him she met at a party.*). We also use underlining to make something stand out, or in typed text use italics to show how *amazed* we are, for example.

It is interesting to note that e-mail and text message communication have come up with a collection of **emoticons** (sometimes called 'smileys') to add more meaning and nuance to otherwise potentially ambiguous language. Thus :-) indicates a smile and shows that the message should not be taken seriously, as in *You must be mad.* :-), whereas :-(suggests sadness, as in *Sorry I can't come to your party.* :-(.

Because writers have fewer paralinguistic devices at their command than speakers in face-to-face interactions, there is a need to be absolutely clear and unambiguous. Frequently readers can't go back to a writer and question what a sentence means or how it should be read. Instead we argue about the meaning of a literary text, or fight each other in the courts because we understand the words of a contract to mean something different from the construction put on them by our opponents.

The product

If we consider a face-to-face conversation to be a 'work in progress' (because through questioning, interrupting, and reformulating we can constantly change the messages being given out), writing usually turns up as a finished product. Whereas we are extremely tolerant of error (and stumbles and reformulations) when talking and listening to someone, the same generosity does not seem to extend to the written form. Here we expect the spelling to be correct, the nouns and verbs to agree with each other, and the punctuation and layout to obey certain conventions.

However, the degree to which writers draft and edit their work into a final product depends, as we have seen, on the kind of writing they are doing. It is quite clear that some speaking-like writing has little status as a finished product (like the example of text messaging on page 3), whereas some writing-like speaking (such as a formal speech) does.

Implications for learning and teaching

A consideration of the writing process, and of how speaking and writing are related to each other – especially in a world of changing communication media – is not only of academic interest. It also has implications for the way we teach writing. Many traditional approaches, for example, failed to incorporate the kinds of insight into the writing process that we have been discussing. In some teaching, for example, students write a composition in the classroom which the teacher corrects and hands back the next day covered in red ink. The students put the corrected pieces of work in their folders and rarely look at them again. For many years the teaching of writing focused on the written product rather than on the writing process. In other words, the students' attention was directed to the *what* rather than the *how* of text construction. Product approaches expected the student to only analyse texts in terms of what language they used and how they were constructed. As we shall see in Chapter 2 (and later on) in this book, such a focus can be highly beneficial for many students. However, we also need to concentrate on the process of writing; and in this regard, there are a number of strategies we need to consider:

- **The way we get students to plan** – before getting students to write we can encourage them to think about what they are going to write – by planning the content and sequence of what they will put down on paper (or type into the computer). There are various ways of doing this including, at one end of the scale, **brainstorming** (where students in pairs or groups come up with as many ideas as they can through discussion) to more **guided tasks** where the teacher or the coursebook includes a number of activities which lead students to plan for a forthcoming task. When students are planning we can encourage them to think not just about the content of what they want to say but also about what the purpose of their writing is, and who the audience is they are writing for.

- **The way we encourage them to draft, reflect, and revise** – students who are unused to process-writing lessons will need to be encouraged to reflect on what they have written, learning how to treat first drafts as first attempts and not as finished products. We may want to train them in using and responding to correction symbols. We may offer them revision 'checklists' to use when looking through what they have written with a view to making revisions.

One way of encouraging drafting, reflection, and revision is to have students involved in **collaborative writing**. A pair or group of students working together on a piece of writing can respond to each other's ideas (both in terms of language and content), making suggestions for changes, and so contributing to the success of the finished product.

- **The way we respond to our students' writing** – in order for a process-writing approach to work well, some teachers may need to rethink the way in which they react to their students' work. In place of making corrections to a finished version, they will need, at times, to **respond** to a work-in-progress. This may involve talking with individual students about a first, second, third, or fourth draft, while other members of the group are working on their own. Alternatively, teachers can read through a draft and then make written suggestions about how the text could be reordered. This is especially appropriate, for example, when the class is working in a computer laboratory where teachers can access one student computer at a time from a central console.

  Another possibility is for the teacher to write out their own version of how a section of text might look better. Such **reformulation** will be beneficial to the student who compares their version with their teacher's.

  It is not just teachers who can respond to students' writing. It is often useful to have students look at work done by their colleagues and respond in their own way. Such **peer response** may provide a welcome alternative to the teacher's feedback, as well as offering a fresh perspective on the writing.

Process writing is a way of looking at what people do when they compose written text. We have seen that it is recursive and may involve many changes of direction while the writer chops and changes between the four main process elements. Nevertheless, process writing may not be the answer in every learning situation. Over-emphasis on process elements may lead us into the process trap.

- **The process trap** – one of the problems of process writing is that it takes time. Over-planning can take up too much time and, sometimes, restrict spontaneity and creativity. Working intensively on second and third drafts also requires periods for reflection, editing, and rewriting. If this is being done conscientiously it can be quite a long process.

  There may be occasions when we find that we do not have enough time to pursue this course of action. A lot will depend on the timetable we are teaching to, and how easy it is to carry work over from one lesson to the next. We will have to think about what students are likely to be able to accomplish in a lesson, say, of 50 minutes. We will need to consider how many students we can work with individually in that time.

We will have to consider the implications for us of responding (outside lesson time) to a number of different drafts per student.

We may want, in some lessons, to prompt students into writing as quickly and immediately as possible. This kind of **instant writing** (often used in writing games) helps to develop the students' **writing fluency**, which is also part of writing proficiency, but which is not the same as the drawn-out processes we have been describing.

Process writing is not an easy option for students or teachers. Quite apart from it taking up time, it takes up space (especially in a paper-driven world) and can be problematic for the more disorganised student.

In the case of written and spoken versions of language we noted that though there are often marked differences between certain types of writing and certain types of speaking, on some occasions they can look fairly similar. Students need to have their attention drawn to these similarities and differences. Where appropriate, we may want to show them the transcript of a piece of conversation and compare that, for example, with a more 'written out' version of the same content.

It also seems clear that students of general English need to be presented with a range of writing tasks, including some of those that are more speaking-like. Depending upon who our students are, we may want to show them text messages and have them attempt to write their own using some of the same conventions as British, Australian, or American users do. We may want them to look at the discourse of Internet chat sites so that they can take part in that kind of spontaneous event themselves.

For the same reasons we may want our students to focus on writing-like-speaking. They can be asked to write speeches or approximations of spoken dialogue.

Conclusions

In this chapter we have:
- looked at the origins of writing.
- discussed the importance and desirability of literacy and numeracy, not least because many exams are writing-based!
- detailed the elements of the writing process and shown how they relate to each other.
- discussed the differences between speaking and writing in terms of time and space, participants, process, language and construction, signs and symbols, and the product.
- said that any text can be described as being more speaking-like or writing-like.
- discussed the teaching and learning implications of the writing process, showing how we need to give students more time for planning and editing, and how we may need to respond rather than correct.
- made comments about the implications of speaking-like-writing and writing-like-speaking for the writing classroom, saying that students need to be made aware of the issues and be given exposure to different kinds of text.

Looking ahead
- In the next chapter we will look at how to describe different types and features of writing.
- In Chapter 3 we will discuss the role and status of writing in L2 learning.
- Subsequent chapters will look at different kinds of writing activity.

2 Describing written text

Writing and reading decrease our sense of isolation. They deepen and widen and expand our sense of life; they feed the soul.
Anne Lamott

- Different purposes, different writing
- Differences within a genre
- Text construction
- Cohesion
- Coherence
- Register
- Implications for learning and teaching

Different purposes, different writing

In the previous chapter we suggested that, during the planning phase of the writing process, authors have to focus on the purpose of their writing (amongst other considerations) since this will affect what language they choose and how they use it. The following examples of written text show clearly how different purposes provoke different kinds of writing. The advertisement below, for example, is intended to attract appropriate applicants for a vacancy in a toy library:

Chanworth Toy Library for Children with Special Needs

Toy Librarian

12hrs per week – pay subject to experience

We are seeking an enthusiastic Toy Librarian to work in the Toy Library at the Child Development Centre and within special schools.

This post is subject to a police check.

Closing date 1st October.

Applications in writing with two referees to Judith Kelly, Chairman, Chanworth Toy Library, PO Box 32, Montley Wood, RC3 5WW.

Why has the writer chosen this particular way of designing the advertisement? It could have been worded differently and been constructed in, say, a more narrative-like form. But if it had been, readers might not have instantly recognised its advertising purpose – and so it would not have been effective.

The fact is that the writer, having decided on a purpose (advertising a job), chose to construct the advertisement on the basis of what the members of the community would be familiar with. In other words, members of a **discourse community** – that is people such as readers of this kind of English-language newspaper – know what an advertisement does and should look like, and the writer has taken this into account in order to make sure they recognise what they are reading for what it is.

The letter below succeeds for the same reasons, although it is very different in character. It is typical of its kind (a formal letter of notification). Thus it follows an established construction pattern:

Stating the subject

Acknowledging receipt of a previous letter

Saying what is to be done

Exhorting the letter's recipient to do something

Signing off

The letter uses specialised **topic vocabulary** (e.g. *Notice of Intended Prosecution; alleged traffic offence*) and also employs vocabulary and grammar which ensures its formal **tone** (*I am in receipt of* … ; *Your prompt response would be appreciated*).

Dear Sir,

I refer to the Notice of Intended Prosecution/Section 172 Road Traffic Act 1988 form sent you in relation to an alleged traffic offence.

I am in receipt of your further correspondence and have noted the contents.

I will, on receiving confirmation from the hospital, re-examine your file. If I decide to excuse the penalty, your payment will be refunded and the points removed from your licence.

Your prompt response would be appreciated.

Yours faithfully,

Genres

The intended reader of the letter also recognises instantly what kind of letter it is because it is typical of its kind (both in terms of construction and in choice of language), just as the advertisement was typical of its kind for the same reasons. We call these different writing constructions ('advertisements', 'letters', etc.) **genres**, and we refer to the specific choice of vocabulary within genres as the **register** that the text is written in.

'Newspaper advertisements' and formal 'letters of notification' are not the only genres around, of course. 'Literary fiction' is a genre of English which is different from, say, 'science fiction'. The characteristics of the latter may well differ in a number of ways from the former, and a specific genre may influence the writer's choice of register. 'Newspaper letters' are a recognisable genre, different from the notification letter above and different again from 'holiday postcards' or 'application letters'. 'Scientific reports' represent a genre of writing, just as 'film criticism' is a genre all of its own.

Knowledge of genres (understanding how different purposes are commonly expressed within a discourse community) is only one of the many 'knowledges' or 'competences' that a reader brings to the task of reading, and which a writer assumes the reader will know. Without these 'knowledges' a communication like the notification letter above would have little chance of success.

These 'knowledges' (which we can group under the general heading of **schematic knowledge**) comprise:

* a knowledge of genres
* general world knowledge
* sociocultural knowledge (that is the social and cultural knowledge which members of a particular social group can reasonably be expected to know)
* topic knowledge (that is knowing something about the subject being discussed).

All of this is exemplified in the following newspaper headline taken from *The Observer* newspaper:

Move over, Big Brother. Now politics is the latest reality TV

Because of our knowledge of genres we recognise this collection of words as a newspaper headline. However, in order to make sense of them we need more than this. Someone who did not have the relevant knowledge might need to be told firstly that *reality TV* involves cameras watching people who have been put, on purpose, in difficult situations (as survivors on a desert island, for example) and secondly that the most successful of all these programmes was called *Big Brother*, where contestants were crammed into a house, filmed all the time, and voted out of the house one by one by the viewers. Of course, it might be possible to deduce some of this information: we could, for example, recognise that the capital letters of *Big Brother* suggest that it is the name of something. But members of the discourse community do not have to make that effort because of their shared sociocultural and topic knowledge.

Differences within a genre

Although we can describe newspaper advertisements as a genre, it is clear that not all advertisements within that genre are the same. Clearly a lot will depend on what is being advertised and, in this case, how much advertisements cost – a genre constraint.

Some writers of newspaper advertisements, as we saw in the 'toy librarian' advertisement above, go into considerable detail, even informing readers that applicants will have their names checked by the police (because no one wants undesirable people working with children). Because a written application is necessary, the advertiser has to give an address and other details.

This advertisement from the same newspaper, however, is significantly different in construction. The writer has clearly put together the information as economically as possible, and this is reflected in the way the advertisement is structured. Nor does he need to include much of the information that the designers of the 'toy librarian' piece required. Mark Jones' advertisement contains no 'well-formed' sentence, and does not need to spend a lot of time exhorting readers to contact him. He

> **EXECUTIVE CAR** hire, available for weddings etc. – Call Mark Jones: 09876 123654

merely puts a phone number there, and members of the discourse community who wish to hire a large, smart car for some grand occasion know exactly what to do.

In other words, there are various sub-genres within a genre. Since within each genre and sub-genre we find typical text constructions, it is useful to look at how such constructions can be described.

Text construction

Literature provides us with perfect examples of how a genre constrains writers, imposing construction patterns that help them to express their purpose. The sonnet (a sub-genre of poetry) demonstrates such constraints:

> Let me not to the marriage of true minds
> Admit impediments. Love is not love
> Which alters when it alteration finds,
> Or bends with the remover to remove:
> O, no! It is an ever-fixéd mark,
> That looks on tempests and is never shaken;
> It is the star to every wandering bark,
> Whose worth's unknown, although his height be taken.
> Love's not Time's fool, though rosy lips and cheeks
> Within his bending sickle's compass come;
> Love alters not with his brief hours and weeks,
> But bears it out even to the edge of doom.
> If this be error and upon me proved,
> I never writ, nor no man ever loved.
>
> *Sonnet 116* by William Shakespeare

A sonnet is a fourteen-line poem where each line – in English, at least – usually consists of ten syllables. The subject matter is most often romantic in nature, and there is generally some kind of a pause – or change in thought or subject – after the first eight lines. Interestingly, there are two main rhyme schemes. Shakespeare, perhaps Britain's most prolific sonneteer, wrote using the Elizabethan rhyme scheme (i.e. *a b a b c d c d e f e f g g* – where *a*, in *Sonnet 116*, represents the *minds, finds* rhyme, and *b* represents the *love, remove* rhyme, etc.).

The American poet E.E. Cummings, writing more than 300 years later, also used the sonnet form to compose his own love poem:

---

it may not always be so

it may not always be so;and i say
that if your lips,which i have loved,should touch
another's,and your dear strong fingers clutch
his heart,as mine in time not far away;
if on another's face your sweet hair lay
in such a silence as i know,or such
great writhing words as,uttering overmuch,
stand helplessly before the spirit at bay;

if this should be,i say if this should be—
you of my heart,send me a little word;
that i may go unto him,and take his hands,
saying,Accept all happiness from me.
Then shall i turn my face,and hear one bird
sing terribly afar in the lost lands.

it may not always be so by E.E. Cummings

Interestingly, Cummings' poem is still constrained by the sonnet form (romantic in nature, 14 lines, 10 syllables per line, and a break after the eighth line), but is different in two respects. Firstly, he uses a variation of the Petrarchan rather than Elizabethan rhyme scheme (i.e *a b b a a b b a* followed by two or three other rhymes in the remaining six lines). Secondly, he brings his own idiosyncratic style to bear on the genre; he liked to write using almost no capital letters (thus violating some of poetry's genre constraints at that time). Where he included capital letters he did so sparingly and for poetic effect. In *it may not always be so* we can suppose that the key concepts he wants us to notice, therefore, are *Accept* and *Then*.

The sonnet form demonstrates how a very tightly structured sub-genre constrains the writers within it. But of course sonnet writing and reading is a minority occupation. Much more common are the holiday postcards, for example, which millions of people write every year. The following example is typical of the genre.

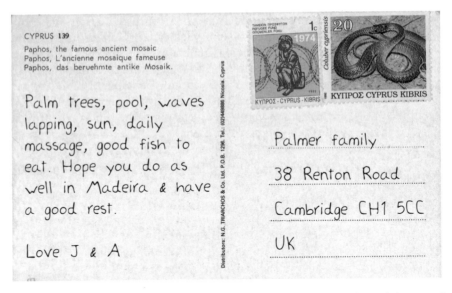

CYPRUS 139

Paphos, the famous ancient mosaic
Paphos, L'ancienne mosaïque fameuse
Paphos, das beruehmte antike Mosaik.

Palm trees, pool, waves
lapping, sun, daily
massage, good fish to
eat. Hope you do as
well in Madeira & have
a good rest.

Love J & A

Palmer family

38 Renton Road

Cambridge CH1 5CC

UK

Just as we were able to describe the construction of the formal letter of notification on page 16, we can also describe the postcard in the same way:

Description of place where the writer is/activities the writer is involved in
(palm trees, waves lapping, daily massage, good fish to eat)

Exhortation to the reader
(Hope you do as well in Madeira & have a good rest.)

Sign off
(Love J & A)

Because postcard writers know this construction pattern, they are able to write cards (such as the one above) at great speed and with great fluency. It takes no time at all to produce a new postcard following the same pattern of construction, such as the example on the right.

Text construction constraints do not only apply to whole texts. Individual paragraphs within a text also tend to follow set patterns. In the example on the next page, few people would have trouble in rearranging the sentences on the left into the properly sequenced paragraph on the right.

That is because even in this kind of narrative the paragraph obeys a common organisational structure, as shown on the next page.

Having great time, expeditions to museums/galleries in the morning, lunch and cerveza followed by siesta, and then down to Plaza Garibaldi to hear the mariachis – and then dinner in a good restaurant. Wish you were here.

Love Amelia

Out-of-sequence sentences	Sequenced paragraph
But then the phone rang, and it was his friend Sarah asking if he wanted to go and see a movie.	Paul was sitting at home, wondering what to do. He didn't have any ideas. But then the phone rang, and it was his friend Sarah asking if he wanted to go and see a movie. He agreed immediately, and was out of the door in almost no time at all.
He agreed immediately, and was out of the door in almost no time at all.	
He didn't have any ideas.	
Paul was sitting at home, wondering what to do.	

Sequencing sentences to make a paragraph

Situation (Paul was sitting at home ...)

⬇

Problem (He didn't have any ideas.)

⬇

Solution/response (But then the phone rang, ...)

⬇

Evaluation/result (He agreed immediately, ...)

As with the holiday postcard, it would not be difficult to write a different paragraph using the same paragraph structure.

There are many different types of paragraph structure, of course. The extract on page 22 from a book about the early days of the Internet does not show the 'problem + solution' shape of the text above about Paul, but instead follows a different pattern:

Topic sentence
(introduces the subject matter of the paragraph)

⬇

Example/explanation sentence
(expands on the information given in the topic sentence)

⬇

Follow-on sentence
(expands on the information given in the example/explanation sentence)

⬇

Conclusion
(ends the paragraph by reminding us of and/or evaluating the opening topic sentence)

> Many people thought that they could make a lot of money from selling goods and services on the Internet. They started up companies called 'dot coms' after the suffixes used in their Internet addresses. They hoped that people would rush to buy online because it would be more convenient. But, for the most part, they did not make the kind of money they expected and, in some cases, they lost everything they had invested.
>
> From *How the Internet Crashed* by Peter Hedley

All text can be analysed in terms of its construction. All genres and sub-genres (of which the sonnet is an extreme example) have relatively strict formulae governing their construction. Business people write letters that are very similar in terms of layout and text organisation even where the content is different. Legal contracts have a standard construction. Wedding invitations follow set construction patterns and so do cooking recipes and car manuals.

When writers put together texts in a particular genre, they follow the constraints of the genre either because they feel obliged to (as in a job application letter) or perhaps because they have got into the habit of doing so (as in a holiday postcard). Of course this does not stop anyone from purposefully violating the genre constraints, as E.E. Cummings does gently in the poem on page 19, but it does help people to write and it helps their readers to digest what they are reading.

For writing to be truly accessible, however, it also needs to be both **cohesive** and **coherent**.

Cohesion   When we write text we have a number of linguistic techniques at our disposal to make sure that our prose 'sticks together'. We can, for example, use lexical repetition and/or 'chains' of words within the same lexical set through a text to have this effect. The topic of the text is reinforced by the use of the same word more than once or by the inclusion of related words (e.g. *water*, *waves*, *sea*, *tide*). We can use various grammatical devices to help the reader understand what is being referred to at all times, even when words are left out or pronouns are substituted for nouns.

We can see lexical and grammatical cohesion at work in the extract from a newspaper article on the page opposite.

Lexical cohesion is achieved in the article by the use of two main devices:

- **Repetition of words** – a number of content words are repeated throughout the text, e.g. *grandparents* (twice), *grandchildren* (twice), *people* (five times), etc.

- **Lexical set 'chains'** – the text is cohesive because there are lexical sets (that is words in the same topic area) which interrelate with each other as the article progresses, e.g. (1) *grandparents, daughters, sons, grandchildren,*

Grandparents 'juggle career and caring'

People in 50s and 60s feel pressure to work on

John Carvel
Social affairs editor

Growing pressure on people in their 50s and 60s to stay in paid work is set to divert grandparents from helping their working daughters and sons with childcare, according to a report today from the Joseph Rowntree Foundation.

It found a shortage of young people in the population – confirmed by the national census on Monday – would make employers do their utmost to retain older staff.

This would shrink the number of retired people who were able to care for their grandchildren or frail older relatives, said researchers from the Institute of Education in London.

After a survey of more than 1,000 employees over 50 and recently retired local authority staff, they identified a 'pivot generation' of people combining work and care roles.

Two-thirds of people between 50 and retirement were in paid employment, one-third had grandchildren by the age of 50, and 60% had living parents.

Nearly half the local authority staff had some caring responsibility. One in three looked after an elderly relative or friend, one in six provided care for a grandchild and one in 10 did both.

From *The Guardian* newspaper – 2.10.02

relatives, grandchild; (2) *work, employers, staff, employees, retired, employment*; (3) *two-thirds, one-third, 60%, one in three, one in 10*; etc.

Grammatical cohesion is achieved in a number of different ways too:

- **Pronoun and possessive reference** – at various points in the text a pronoun or more frequently a possessive is used instead of a noun. In the first sentence (*Growing pressure on people in their 50s and 60s …*) *their* is used to refer back to *people*.

  Like most texts, the article has many examples of such pronoun and possessive reference. The second *their* in paragraph 1 refers back but this time to the noun *grandparents*, whereas *their* in paragraph 2 refers back to *employers*. Such **anaphoric reference** can operate between paragraphs too. *This* which starts paragraph 3 refers back to the whole of paragraph 2, whereas *they* in paragraph 4 refers back to *researchers from the Institute of Education* in the previous paragraph.

- **Article reference** – articles are also used for text cohesion. The definite article (*the*) is often used for anaphoric reference. For example, in paragraph 4 the writer refers to *retired local authority staff*, but when they are mentioned again in paragraph 6 the writer talks about *the local* *authority staff*, and the reader understands that he is talking about the local authority staff who were identified two paragraphs before.

However *the* is not always used in this way. When the writer talks about *the national census*, he assumes his readers will know what he is referring to and that there is only one of it. Such **exophoric reference** assumes a world knowledge shared by the discourse community who the piece is written for.

- **Tense agreement** – writers use tense agreement to make texts cohesive. In our 'grandparents' article the past tense predominates (*It found*) and what is sometimes called the 'future-in-the-past' (*would make*) also occurs. If, on the other hand, the writer was constantly changing tense, the text would not hold together in the same way.

- **Linkers** – texts also achieve coherence through the use of **linkers** – words describing text relationships of 'addition' (*and, also, moreover, furthermore*), of 'contrast' (*however, on the other hand, but, yet*), of 'result' (*therefore, consequently, thus*), of 'time' (*first, then, later, after a while*), etc.

- **Substitution and ellipsis** – writers frequently substitute a short phrase for a longer one that has preceded it, in much the same way as they use pronoun reference (see above). For example, in *He shouldn't have cheated in his exam but he **did so** because he was desperate to get into university* the phrase *did so* substitutes for *cheated in his exam*. Writers use ellipsis (where words are deliberately left out of a sentence when the meaning is still clear) in much the same way. For example, in *Penny was introduced to a famous author, but even before she was she had recognised him* the second clause omits the unnecessary repetition of *introduced to a famous author*.

Coherence   The cohesive devices we have discussed help to bind elements of a text together so that we know what is being referred to and how the phrases and sentences relate to each other. But it is perfectly possible to construct a text which, although it is rich in such devices, makes little sense because it is not coherent. The following example is fairly cohesive but it is not terribly coherent:

> This made her afraid. It was open at the letters page. His eyes were shut and she noticed the *Daily Mail* at his side. She knew then that he had read her contribution. Gillian came round the corner of the house and saw her husband sitting in his usual chair on the terrace. She wished now that she had never written to the paper.

As we can see, for a text to have coherence, it needs to have some kind of internal logic which the reader can follow with or without the use of prominent cohesive devices. When a text is coherent, the reader can understand at least two things:

- **The writer's purpose** – the reader should be able to understand what the writer's purpose is. Is it to give information, suggest a course of action, make a judgement on a book or play, or express an opinion about world events, for example? A coherent text will not mask the writer's purpose.

- **The writer's line of thought** – the reader should be able to follow the writer's line of reasoning if the text is a discursive piece. If, on the other hand, it is a narrative, the reader should be able to follow the story and not get confused by time jumps, or too many characters, etc. In a descriptive piece the reader should know what is being described and what it looks, sounds, smells, or tastes like.

  Good instruction manuals show coherence at work so that the user of the manual can clearly follow step-by-step instructions and therefore complete the assembly or procedure successfully. Where people complain about instruction manuals it is often because they are not written coherently enough.

Coherence, therefore, is frequently achieved by the way in which a writer sequences information, and this brings us right back to the issue of genre and text construction. It is precisely because different genres provoke different writing (in order to satisfy the expectations of the discourse community that is being written for) that coherence is achieved. When writers stray outside text construction norms, coherence is one of the qualities that is most at risk. Indeed our description of paragraph constructions on page 21 is, more than anything else, a demonstration of how coherence is achieved.

However, it must not be assumed that genre constraints serve to stifle creativity – or that the need for coherence implies a lack of experimentation. Whether or not writers choose to accept or violate genre constraints (and thereby, perhaps affect the coherence of their texts) is up to them.

Register The text below is an example of the 'sleeve-note' genre – the musical description which comes with CDs to explain what the listener will hear (in this case Mahler's *9th Symphony*). Non-musical readers, while recognising the names of instruments (e.g. *cello, harp, horn, viola*), might have more difficulty with terms such as *sparsely scored, syncopated rhythm, sextuplet*, but these are easily understood by those who are familiar with music terminology:

> Mahler first presents, in a brief and sparsely scored introduction, four very basic ideas which assume importance throughout the movement: the cellos' and horns' opening syncopated rhythm (three notes); the harp's first strident four notes; five notes played by muted horn; and an accompanimental flutter – a sextuplet – played by the violas.

From the sleeve-note for Mahler's *9th Symphony* by Stephen Petit, Philips records

These sleeve-notes are written in a particular type of musical **register** which we might describe as 'classical' and 'academic'. Register is a word used to denote the actual language that we use in a particular situation when communicating with a particular group of people. Once a genre has been chosen and identified, it is the register the writer chooses that determines the choice of words. Texts in the same genre, therefore, can be written in different registers: the sleeve-notes for a new album from Eminem or Christina Aguilera will probably be written in a different register, one from the other, and certainly from the words accompanying a new recording of works by Bach or Handel. However, the more closely a sub-genre is identified (i.e. 'classical music sleeve-notes') the more likely it is that the genre will determine what register the piece is written in.

One aspect of register is the choice of **topic vocabulary**. In the case of the Mahler text, phrases like *sparsely scored*, *muted horn*, and *accompanimental flutter* exemplify this kind of choice. They would not be used in notes for a pop record, nor would they be found in a scientific journal or a computer manual.

Register, then, involves the choice of topic vocabulary to suit the subject matter of the piece. However, register is not just about topic-vocabulary choice. It is also about the **tone** of a piece – how formal or informal it is. The advertisement below, for example, is clearly designed for sophisticated readers using, as it does, descriptive words such as *entrancing*, *merest hint*, and *gentle restraint*. These are distancing words in some ways, appealing to cool and elegant readers who aspire to the poise and beauty which the *Essenzia* product will hopefully bestow on them.

New look for a new year
Possibility ...

For a delicate entrancing look, dust your eyes with the merest hint of colour. Suggest shades for your lips and nails with gentle restraint. Suffuse your face with possibility.

Be sophisticated, be subtle.

Be mysterious, be mesmerising.

Be you ...

ESSENZIA
We explore beauty, quietly.

GOOD NIGHT OUT?

Here are our top tips for a good night out:

1 Don't wear skimpy clobber. You'll catch your death. Splash out on a cosy jumper. Cover your legs and they'll stop shaking!

2 Too much tonsil tennis can be confusing. Much better to keep the lads guessing and your head clear.

3 Ease up on the slap. We all like a bit of lippy and there's nothing wrong with blusher or shadow, but you don't want to look like a neon sign!

However, the extract above, which comes from a magazine for young teenagers, is written in an entirely different register, even though it touches on similar topics (e.g. appearance and make-up).

The vocabulary in this piece reflects a significantly less formal or distanced tone than in the previous example. Terms like *skimpy clobber, tonsil tennis, lads, ease up on the slap* (= use less make-up), and *lippy* (= lipstick) are all slang terms which were current when the piece was written. Such words and expressions are of their time, and are used informally between (young) friends. The topic has determined the vocabulary, in other words, but so has the tone which the writer wished to use to communicate with the audience.

Implications for learning and teaching

We have seen that writing in a particular genre tends to lead to the use of certain kinds of text construction. This must have implications not only for the way people write in their first or main language, but also for the ways in which we teach people to become better writers in a foreign language. Since people write in different registers depending on different topics and on the tone they wish to adopt for their intended audience, then students need to be made aware of how this works in English so that they too can choose language appropriately. If, for example, a class of people studying business English need to learn how to write job application letters, then clearly they will need to know how, typically, such application letters are put together and what register they are written in – something that will depend, often, on the kind of job they are applying for. If our students wish to learn how to write discursive essays for some exam, then it follows that they will benefit from knowing how, typically, such essays are constructed.

Students will also benefit greatly from learning how to use cohesive devices effectively and from being prompted to give a significant amount of attention to coherent organisation within a genre.

It would be impossible to explain different genre constructions or to demonstrate text cohesion devices without letting students see examples of the kind of writing we wish them to aim for. Writing within genres in the language classroom implies, therefore, a significant attention to reading.

- **Reading and writing** – students might well enjoy writing 'lonely hearts' advertisements for example. It would, anyway, provide vocabulary practice but it might also allow them to be imaginative and, hopefully, have some fun. However, the only way to get them to do this is to let them read examples of the kind of thing we want them to do before we ask them to write.

If we ask our students to read 'lonely hearts' advertisements (because, later, we are going to ask them to write their own versions), we can ask them to analyse the texts they have in front of them. In order to draw their attention to the way the texts are structured, we might ask them to put the following genre elements in the order they occur in the texts:

Contact instruction (e.g. *Write Box 2562*)
Description of advertiser (e.g. *Good-looking 35-year-old rock climber and music lover*)
Description of desired responder (e.g. *young woman with similar interests*)
For (description of activities/desired outcome) (e.g. *for relaxation, fun, friendship*)
'Would like to meet' (e.g. *WLTM*)

We can then ask them to find the language which is used for each element. Now, as a result of reading and analysing a text (or texts – e.g. a number of different advertisements of the same type) they are in a position to have a go at writing in the same genre themselves.

Obviously, we would only ask students to write 'lonely hearts' advertisements for fun. When we ask them to write a business letter, however, we will do so because we think they may need to write such letters in the future. Thus we will let them read a variety of letters, drawing their attention to features of layout (e.g. where the addresses go, how the date is written). We will make sure they recognise features of text construction (e.g. how business letters often start, what the relationship between the paragraphs is, how business-letter writers sign off) and language use (e.g. what register the letters are written in). We may also have students analyse the letters to spot examples of cohesive language. They will then be in a position to write their own similar letters obeying the same genre constraints and employing at least some of the same language.

We do not have to tell the students everything. We can, for example, get them to look at five or six versions of the same news story. It will be their job to identify any similarities of construction and to find the vocabulary items and phrases which occur on more than two occasions. They will then be able to use these when writing their own similar newspaper articles.

At lower levels (e.g. beginners and elementary), we may not be able to expect that students can analyse complete texts and then go on to write imitations of them. But we can, through **parallel writing**, get them to look at a paragraph, for example, and then, having discussed its structure, write their own similar ones. By using the same paragraph construction (see page 21) and some of the same vocabulary, they can, even at this early stage, write well-formed paragraphs in English.

In other words, where students are asked to write within a specific genre, a prerequisite for their successful completion of the task will be to read and analyse texts written within that same genre.

However, there is a danger in concentrating too much on the study and analysis of different genres. Over-emphasis may lead us into the genre trap.

• **The genre trap** – if we limit students to imitating what other people have written, then our efforts may end up being **prescriptive** (you must do it like this) rather than **descriptive** (for your information, this is how it is often done). Students may feel that the only way they can write a text or a paragraph is to slavishly imitate what they have been studying. Yet writing is a creative undertaking whether we are designing an advertisement or putting up a notice in school. Unless we are careful, an emphasis on text construction and language use may lead to little more than text 'reproduction'.

A focus on genre can avoid these pitfalls if we ensure that students understand that the examples they read are **examples** rather than **models** to be slavishly followed. This is more difficult at beginner level, however, where students may well want to stick extremely closely to paragraph models.

A way out of this dilemma is to make sure that students see a number of examples of texts within a genre, especially where the examples all have individual differences. This will alert students to the descriptive rather than prescriptive nature of genre analysis. Thus when students look at newspaper advertisements, we will show them a variety of different types. We will make sure they see a variety of different recipes (if they are going to write recipes of their own) so that they both recognise the similarities between them, but also become aware of how, sometimes, their construction is different. For each genre that they encounter, in other words, we will try to ensure a **variety of exposure** so that they are not tied to one restrictive model.

We will also need to accept that genre analysis and writing is not the only kind of writing that students (or teachers) need or want to do. On the contrary, we may often encourage students to write about themselves, including stories about what they have done recently. Sometimes, in our lessons, we should get students to write short essays, compositions, or dialogues straight out of their heads with no reference to genre at all.

We need to remind ourselves that understanding a genre and writing within it is only one part of the picture for our students. As we saw in Chapter 1, we can help them enormously if we focus on the actual process of writing. Reconciling a concentration on genre with the desirability of involving students in the writing process – and finding a balance between the two – will be a major theme of the rest of this book.

Conclusions

In Chapter 2 we have:
- described writing in terms of genre.
- discussed what genre means and looked at examples of texts within certain genres.
- shown how, even within one genre, there can be varieties of text construction.
- analysed a number of texts in terms of their construction, showing how strict genre formats can both constrain and stimulate authors.
- seen examples of cohesive devices within a text.
- discussed the issue of coherence.
- seen how writers choose their words depending on genre, topic, and tone.
- said that genre analysis implies that students should read before they write so that they can see how texts are organised and what language is used.
- pointed out, however, that if written genres are used only for students to copy slavishly then they may be counter-productive. A sensible approach to genre, therefore, is to show students many examples within a genre and to use genre studies in conjunction with other kinds of writing activity.

Looking ahead

- In the next chapter we will discuss the role and status of writing in the L2 classroom and discuss the different ways in which students can be asked to write.
- Subsequent chapters will look at different kinds of writing activity.

3 Writing in the language classroom

Most people won't realize that writing is a craft. You have to take your apprenticeship in it like anything else.
Katherine Ann Porter

- **Writing for learning**
- **Writing for writing**
- **The tasks of the teacher in writing**

Writing for learning

Writing (as one of the four skills of listening, speaking, reading, and writing) has always formed part of the syllabus in the teaching of English. However, it can be used for a variety of purposes, ranging from being merely a 'backup' for grammar teaching to a major syllabus strand in its own right, where mastering the ability to write effectively is seen as a key objective for learners.

The importance given to writing differs from teaching situation to teaching situation. In some cases it shares equal billing with the other skills; in other curricula it is only used, if at all, in its 'writing-for-learning' role where students write predominantly to augment their learning of the grammar and vocabulary of the language.

Partly because of the nature of the writing process and also because of the need for accuracy in writing, the mental processes that a student goes through when writing differ significantly from the way they approach discussion or other kinds of spoken communication. This is just as true for single-sentence writing as it is with single paragraphs or extended texts. As we saw in Chapter 1, writing is often not time-bound in the way conversation is. When writing, students frequently have more time to think than they do in oral activities. They can go through what they know in their minds, and even consult dictionaries, grammar books, or other reference material to help them. Writing encourages students to focus on accurate language use and, because they think as they write, it may well provoke language development as they resolve problems which the writing puts into their minds. However, this is quite separate from the issues of writing process and genre that we discussed in the first two chapters, since here students are not writing to become better writers. They are writing to help them learn better.

Reinforcement writing

Writing has always been used as a means of reinforcing language that has been taught. In its simplest form, teachers often ask students to write sentences using recently learnt grammar. Suppose, for example, that intermediate students have recently been practising the third conditional (*If + had (not) done + would (not) have done*), they might be given the following instruction:

> **Write two sentences about things you wish had turned out differently, and two sentences about things you are pleased about.**

The teacher hopes, then, that students will write sentences such as:

> (things you wish had turned out differently)
>
> If I hadn't failed my exams, I would have gone to university.
>
> (things you are pleased about)
>
> If I hadn't gone to that party, I wouldn't have met my boyfriend.

The same kind of sentence writing can be used to get students to practise or research vocabulary, as the following exercise shows:

> **Write a sentence about a friend or a member of your family using at least two of these character adjectives: *proud, kind, friendly, helpful, impatient* ...**

Reinforcement writing need not be confined to sentence writing, however. Students can also be asked to write paragraphs or longer compositions to practise certain recently focused-on aspects of language or paragraph and text construction. Students might be asked to write a story about something that happened to them (or that is based on a character or events in their coursebook) as a good way of having them practise past tenses. They could be asked to write a description of someone they know because this is a good way of getting them to use the character and physical description vocabulary they have been studying.

Clearly the aim of these activities is to give students opportunities to remember 'new' language better. Just the act of writing sentences makes them think about the new grammar or vocabulary in a more considered way than if we asked them to provide instant spoken examples.

Preparation writing

Writing is frequently useful as preparation for some other activity, in particular when students write sentences as a preamble to discussion activities. This gives students time to think up ideas rather than having to come up with instant fluent opinions, something that many, especially at lower levels, find difficult and awkward.

Students may be asked to write a sentence saying what their opinion is about a certain topic. For example, they may be asked to complete sentences such as:

I like/don't like going to parties because …

This means that when the class as a whole is asked to talk about going to parties they can either read out what they have written, or use what they thought as they wrote, to make their points.

Another technique, when a discussion topic is given to a class, is for students to talk in groups to prepare their arguments. They can make written notes which they may use later during the discussion phase.

In these cases, where writing has been used as preparation for something else, it is an immensely enabling skill even though it is not the main focus of an activity.

Activity writing

Writing can also, of course, be used as an integral part of a larger activity where the focus is on something else such as language practice, acting out, or speaking. Teachers often ask students to write short dialogues which they will then act out. The dialogues are often most useful if planned to practise particular functional areas, such as inviting or suggesting. Students work in pairs to make the dialogue and, where possible, the teacher goes to help them as they write. They now have something they can read out or act out in the class.

Writing is also used in questionnaire-type activities. Groups of students may be asked to design a questionnaire, for example about the kind of music people like. The teacher then asks them all to stand up and circulate around the class asking their colleagues the questions they have previously prepared. They write down the answers and then report back to the class on what they have found out.

Once again, writing is used to help students perform a different kind of activity (in this case speaking and listening). Students need to be able to write to do these activities, but the activities do not teach students to write.

Writing for writing

It will be clear from the above that not all writing activities necessarily help students to write more effectively, or, if they do, that is a by-product of the activity rather than its main purpose. However, the 'writing-for-learning' activities we have discussed so far do depend on the students' ability to write already. There is no attempt to teach a new writing skill or show students how to work in unfamiliar genres, for example.

Teaching 'writing for writing' is entirely different, however, since our objective here is to help students to become better writers and to learn how to write in various genres using different registers. General language improvement may, of course, occur, but that is a by-product of a 'writing-for-writing' activity, not necessarily its main purpose. The kind of writing teaching with which this book is mostly concerned is quite separate and distinct from the teaching of grammatical or lexical accuracy and range, even though both may improve as a result of it.

Although, as we shall see in the next chapter, it is important to help students with matters of **handwriting**, **orthography** (the spelling system), and **punctuation**, teaching writing is more than just dealing with these features too. It is about helping students to communicate real messages in an appropriate manner.

Example lesson (intermediate)

The following example shows a 'writing-for-writing' procedure where language is put at the service of a skill and a specific task, and where features such as layout and language choice − including issues of register − are focused on to help students write better in a particular genre or genres. It is in six stages, with students doing their own writing, initially working at the board in a collaborative writing process and later writing their own letters.

- **Stage 1** − the students first read the letter on the opposite page and answer the following questions about it:

> a   Where is Brenda writing from?
> b   How did she and Mariel get there?
> c   How did she feel when she first arrived? How does she feel now?
> d   What differences are there between Brenda's and Mariel's character?
> e   What is Brenda's job? What is Mariel's?
> f   Who is David?
> g   How formal is the letter? How do you know?

When the students have read the letter and answered the questions, they discuss features of an informal and friendly letter like this one, such as where the sender's address is normally written and how the date is written.

- **Stage 2** − the students are then asked to choose either I (informal), F (formal), or N (neutral) for the following letter phrases.

Flat 3
156 Centenary Road,
Mumbai,
India

June 15th

Dear Rosemary,

I've just received your letter – thanks. It was nice to hear from you.

Well, we've been here for three weeks already. I still can't believe it. But things have definitely improved since the bus left us at the roadside on that first day. For a minute I wanted to turn round and go home again. You know me, I'm a great pessimist. But Mariel always thinks everything is going to be fine. In less than a day she had found us a flat and here we are.

I've found myself a job giving private conversation classes. Not quite what I'm used to, but it's still teaching and my students are lovely. Mariel hasn't got a job yet, but she's made contact with various people in the film industry here and hopes she'll get work soon.

So the big news is, we've made our decision. We've decided to stay. This is our home.

Please give my love to David and the kids. Why not come and visit us soon?

Lots of love,
Brenda

A letter from *Just Right: intermediate* by Jeremy Harmer

a	Hi Rosemary,	I / F / N
b	Dear Mrs Forrest,	I / F / N
c	Dear James,	I / F / N
d	Dear Ms Forrest,	I / F / N
e	Dear Sir or Madam,	I / F / N
f	With best wishes,	I / F / N
g	Lots of love,	I / F / N
h	Yours sincerely,	I / F / N
i	Yours faithfully,	I / F / N
j	Love,	I / F / N
k	Thanks for your letter.	I / F / N
l	Thank you very much for your letter.	I / F / N
m	Please give my love to David and the kids.	I / F / N
n	I look forward to hearing from you.	I / F / N

- **Stage 3** – now that they have looked at features of genre and register in letter writing, it is time for them to put what they have discussed into practice. The teacher puts an invitation on the overhead projector:

The teacher then draws two squares on the board to one side of the projected invitation:

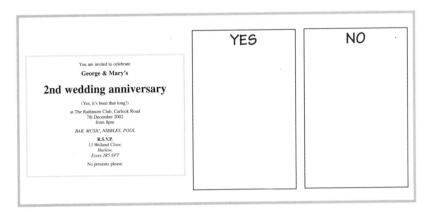

- **Stage 4** – students then go up to the board one by one and write first the address and date and then individual lines for the 'yes' and 'no' letters, using suggestions made by their colleagues and by the teacher. If a student puts the address in the wrong place, the students or the teacher help her to reposition it. The teacher may elicit the expression *I'm afraid* for the 'no' letter if the student at the board does not think of it. There may be a discussion about different ways of writing the date, and the class can discuss the difference (in register and appropriacy) between *Thank you* and *Thanks* for example. This is process writing in miniature, each sentence being drafted and rewritten collaboratively, just as, in a more extensive sequence, students might plan and draft text which they then revise and re-draft on the basis of comment from the teacher or students.

Here are two letters that were written in this way:

28 Mill Road, Cambridge CB1 3NL Nov. 12th Dear Mary & George, Thank you very much for your invitation. I would love to come to your party. I look forward to seeing you on the 7th. Lots of love, Mi Sook	7 Lilac Court, Cherry Hinton, Cambridge CB1 2XG Nov. 13th Dear Mary and George, Thanks for your invitation but I'm afraid I won't be able to come because I promised to go to my grandfather's birthday party. I hope you have a wonderful evening. I look forward to seeing you soon. Best regards, Rose

Student-constructed board letters

- **Stage 5** – students can then be asked to look at a new letter with gaps in it, as shown on the next page. The students complete the text by adding one word for each gap. When they have done this the teacher can go through the answers before leading a discussion about the differences between this (business/application) letter and the letters they had previously seen and written, such as whether or not the recipients' address is included.

- **Stage 6** – finally, students can write a letter for homework in response to an advertisement, like the one on the next page.

  Because students have had a chance to study different examples of letters and because they have discussed how they might replicate some of their features, they are in a good position to complete the homework task.

  When the teacher receives the homework he or she can respond to it by saying where it has succeeded and by making suggestions for re-drafting and rewriting. Students can then produce a final version.

17 Hillside Road
Chesswood
Herts. WD3 5LB
Tel 01923 284171
Fax 01923 286622

Thursday 17 January

David Benton
Worldwatch UK Ltd
357 Ferry Rd
Basingstoke RG2 5HP

Dear Mr Benton

I saw your .... for a Business Journalist in today's Guardian newspaper. I am very .... in the job and I think that I have many of the necessary ....

I .... politics and modern languages at Oxford University. I am .... in French, German and Spanish. I have .... widely in Europe and South America, and I .... worked as a business journalist for the BBC .... the last five years.

I enclose a copy of my Curriculum Vitae. I look forward .... hearing from you soon. Please let me know if you need more information.

Yours sincerely

Nancy Mann

Nancy Mann

From *New Headway Intermediate* by John and Liz Soars

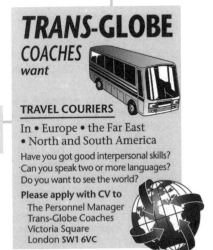

The procedure outlined in the previous five pages shows how a skill-focused lesson differs significantly from a sequence devoted exclusively, for example, to general language improvement. Here writing (in this case letter writing) was at the heart of the lesson, and was its primary focus rather than acting as an adjunct to other activities.

Writing purposes

When teaching 'writing for writing' we need to make sure that our students have some writing aim. As we saw in Chapter 2, effective writers usually have a purpose in mind and construct their writing with a view to achieving that purpose.

The most effective learning of writing skills is likely to take place when students are writing real messages for real audiences, or at least when they are performing tasks which they are likely to have to do in their out-of-class life. The choice of writing tasks will depend, therefore, on why students are studying English. There are three main categories of learning which it is worth considering:

- **English as a Second Language (ESL)** – this term is normally used to describe students who are living in the target language community and who need English to function in that community on a day-to-day basis. Recent immigrants and refugees, for example, will have specific writing needs such as the ability to fill in a range of forms, or write particular kinds of letters (depending upon their exact needs and circumstances), alongside the need for general English development.

- **English for Specific Purposes (ESP)** – many students study English for a particular (or specific) purpose. People who are going to work as nurses in Britain or the USA, for example, will study medical English. Those who are going to study at an English-medium university need to concentrate on English for Academic Purposes (EAP). Business students will concentrate on the language of management and commerce, and so on.

  The choice of topics and tasks for such students should not only develop their general language competence but also be relevant to their reason for study. For example, writing tasks for business students can have a high **face validity** if the students can see that they are writing the kind of letters and documents which they will be writing in their professional life. Likewise nurses in training, when asked to write up a simulated patient record in their English class, will clearly see the value of such a task.

- **English as a Foreign Language (EFL)** – this is generally taken to apply to students who are studying general English at schools and institutes in their own country or as transitory visitors in a target-language country. Their needs are often not nearly so easy to pin down as the two categories we have mentioned above.

  While it is perfectly possible to ask school students what their needs are or will be, it is unlikely that it will be easy to make a list of any but the most general aims. In the case of adult students, it is often hard to find writing tasks that are directly relevant to the varying needs of a class full of students from different backgrounds and occupations. Nevertheless, it may well be possible to arrive at a set of tasks that are a useful compromise between the competing claims of the individuals in a class.

The best thing we can do is to concentrate on a repertoire of writing tasks that it is reasonable to assume that most speakers of English may have to take part in at some stage in their English-speaking lives. Most of such writing activities fall on a cline somewhere between **real purpose** versus **invented purpose** tasks. Real purpose tasks are precisely the ones that we can predict our students will probably need to perform at some stage. The letters we looked at in this chapter (on pages 35–38) fall near the 'real purpose' end of our cline since it is likely that our students will, at some stage, have to write formal and semi-formal letters of the same type. Similarly, we might well get our students to look at the language of e-mails and have them practise writing their own, or get them to write a report of a process or situation.

Invented purposes, on the other hand, are those which, however engaging, are unlikely to be directly relevant to our students' future needs. A popular activity in many classrooms is to have students write letters to imaginary magazine problem pages and then have other students reply in the guise of 'agony aunts'. Students will probably never need to write 'agony' letters in English, but such an activity will provoke them into thinking about how to best express themselves in writing, and how to format a letter, for example. In the same way as we saw on page 28, we might have students look at the kind of 'lonely hearts' advertisements that appear in many newspapers and magazines, not because our students will need to write such advertisements, but because by looking at them with a quizzical eye they can develop their **genre-analysing habits**. This, in turn, may help them to write the kind of telegraphic writing that is common in advertisements and newspaper headlines. On top of that, if students find the activity amusing and engaging it will help to build in them a positive attitude to writing (a skill often viewed with less enthusiasm than, say, speaking).

One other skill needs to be discussed here, and that is **exam writing**. Although many tests are becoming computerised and heavily reliant on multiple-choice questions, many still have a writing component designed to discover the candidate's **integrative** language abilities – that is, their ability to write texts displaying correct grammar, appropriate lexis, and coherent organisation. Integrative test items (which ask students to display all these skills) are different from **discrete test items** where only one thing, for example a grammar point, is tested at one time. Whereas the former test 'writing for writing', the latter use writing only as a medium for language testing.

Creative writing

Creative writing is one area (like painting and composing) where the imagination has a chance to run free. The world is full of people who achieve great personal satisfaction in this way. In their book *Process Writing*, the authors Ron White and Valerie Arndt describe an approach that 'views all writing – even the most mundane and routine – as creative'. Such an approach would even include, at some level, the putting together of a shopping list (see page 4). But we are concerned here with tasks that provoke students to go beyond the everyday, and which ask them to spread their linguistic wings, take some chances, and use the language they are learning to express more personal or more complex thoughts and images. We can ask them to write stories or poems, to write journals, or to create dramatic scenarios. This will not be easy, of course, because of the limitations many students come up against when writing in the L2. Nor will all students respond well to the invitation to be ambitious and to take risks. But for some, the provision of genuinely creative tasks may open up avenues they have not previously travelled down either in the L1 or the L2.

Creative writing tasks are nearer the 'invented purpose' end of our purpose cline, but they can still be very motivating since they provide opportunities for students to display their work – to show off, in other words, in a way that speaking often does not. The writing they produce can be pinned up on notice-boards, collected in class folders or magazines, or put up as a page on a class site on a school intranet or on the World Wide Web itself. Nor should we forget that this use of writing is one of the few occasions that students write for a wider audience; for once it may not just be the teacher who will read their work.

The tasks of the teacher in writing

When helping students to become better writers, teachers have a number of crucial tasks to perform. This is especially true when students are doing 'writing-for-writing' activities, where they may be reluctant to express themselves or have difficulty finding ways and means of expressing themselves to their satisfaction.

Among the tasks which teachers have to perform before, during, and after student writing are the following:

- **Demonstrating** – since, as we have said, students need to be aware of writing conventions and genre constraints in specific types of writing, teachers have to be able to draw these features to their attention. In whatever way students are made aware of layout issues or the language used to perform certain written functions, for example, the important issue is that they are made aware of these things – that these things are drawn to their attention.

- **Motivating and provoking** – student writers often find themselves 'lost for words', especially in creative writing tasks. This is where the teacher can help, provoking the students into having ideas, enthusing them with the value of the task, and persuading them what fun it can be. It helps, for example, if teachers go into class with prepared suggestions so that when students get stuck they can immediately get help rather than having, themselves, to think of ideas on the spot. Time spent preparing amusing and engaging ways of getting students involved in a particular writing task will not be wasted. Students can be asked to complete tasks on the board or reassemble jumbled texts as a prelude to writing; they can be asked to exchange 'virtual' e-mails or discuss ideas before the writing activity starts. Sometimes teachers can give them the words they need to start a writing task as a way of getting them going.

- **Supporting** – closely allied to the teacher's role as motivator and provoker is that of supporting. Students need a lot of help and reassurance once they get going, both with ideas and with the means to carry them out. Teachers need to be extremely supportive when students are writing in class, always available (except during exam writing of course), and prepared to help students overcome difficulties.

- **Responding** – the way we react to students' written work can be divided into two main categories, that of responding and that of evaluating. When responding, we react to the content and construction of a piece supportively and often (but not always) make suggestions for its improvement. When we respond to a student's work at various draft stages, we will not be grading the work or judging it as a finished product. We will, instead, be telling the student how well it is going so far.

  When students write journals (see Chapter 8) we may respond by reacting to what they have said (e.g. 'Your holiday sounds very interesting, Silvia. I liked the bit about running out of petrol but I didn't understand exactly who went and got some petrol. Could you possibly write and tell me in your next journal entry?') rather than filling their journal entry full of correction symbols. We might also make comments about their use of language and suggest ways of improving it (e.g. 'Be careful with your past tenses, Nejati. Look at the verbs I've underlined and see if you can write them correctly.') but this is done as part of a process rather than part of an evaluation procedure.

- **Evaluating** – there are many occasions, however, when we do want to evaluate students' work, telling both them and us how well they have done. All of us want to know what standard we have reached (in the case of a **progress/achievement** test). When evaluating our students' writing for test purposes, we can indicate where they wrote well and where they made mistakes, and we may award grades; but, although test-marking is different from responding, we can still use it not just to grade students but also as a learning opportunity. When we hand back marked scripts we can get our students to look at the errors we have highlighted and try to put them right – rather than simply stuffing the corrected pieces of work into the back of their folders and never looking at them again.

Conclusions

In this chapter we have:
- divided writing into two categories: 'writing for learning' and 'writing for writing'.
- said that it is in 'writing for writing' that students are able to study written text in order to become better writers (in English) themselves.
- looked at a detailed writing sequence to show how a series of tasks – from looking at how something is written, through practice to a final task – help to teach writing within a specific genre or genres.
- looked at different writing purposes in the light of the students' reasons for studying English.

- shown how tasks fall on a cline between real and invented purposes.
- discussed the value of creative writing.
- discussed the teacher tasks of demonstrating, motivating, supporting, responding, and evaluating.

Looking ahead
- In the next chapter we will be looking at the nuts and bolts of writing – how to teach writing conventions, how to help students generate ideas, etc.
- In Chapter 5 we will look at how to build the writing habit through tasks which encourage students to write fluently and with gusto.
- In Chapter 6 we will look at more extended writing tasks and in Chapter 7 we will show how teachers should respond to such tasks.

4 Nuts and bolts

We are all apprentices in a craft where no one ever becomes a master.
Ernest Hemingway

- The mechanics of writing
- The handwriting challenge
- Teaching handwriting
- The spelling challenge
- Teaching spelling
- Teaching punctuation
- Copying
- Sentence, paragraph, and text

The mechanics of writing

Writing, like any other skill, has its 'mechanical' components. These include handwriting, spelling, punctuation, and the construction of well-formed sentences, paragraphs, and texts. Such things are the nuts and bolts of the writing skill and they need to be focused on at certain stages of learning to write in English. The greater the difference between the student's L1 and English, in some or all of these areas, the bigger the challenge for student and teacher alike.

The activities in this chapter – which are designed to help students overcome problems with handwriting and spelling, for example – are enabling exercises on the way to developing an overall writing ability. Similarly, the techniques which are described here, such as **copying** and **parallel writing** (imitating a written model), help to give students a basic mechanical competence which they can then put to use when they write more creatively.

The handwriting challenge

Although a lot of writing is typed on computer keyboards, handwriting is still necessary and widespread, whether in exam writing, postcards, forms (such as application forms), etc. It should be remembered too, that however fast computer use is growing it is still, in world terms, a minority occupation.

Handwriting can be particularly difficult for some students. For those who are brought up using characters such as in Chinese or Japanese, or using very different scripts such as in Arabic or Indonesian, writing in Roman **cursive** or 'joined-up' lettering presents a number of problems.

Areas of difficulty can include producing the shapes of English letters, not only in **upper case** (capitals) but also in their **lower case** (non-capital) equivalents. The relative size of individual letters in a word or text can cause problems, as can their correct positioning with or without ruled lines.

For students accustomed in their L1 to writing from right to left, Western script, which of course goes in the opposite direction, can involve not only problems of perception but also necessitates a different angle and position for the writing arm.

Teaching handwriting

For students who have trouble with some or all of the above aspects of English handwriting, teachers can follow a two-stage approach which involves first the recognition and then the production of letters.

Recognition

If students are to form English letters correctly, they have to recognise them first. For example, they can be asked to recognise specific letters within a sequence of letters. Subsequently, they can focus on recognising specific strings of letters, as in this example:

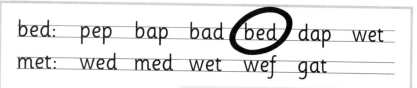

bed: pep bap bad (bed) dap wet

met: wed med wet wef gat

'Letter-string' recognition from www.eltlinks.co.uk

The teacher can draw letters or words in the air which students have to identify. Students can 'write' a word on a fellow student's back (or hand) which that student has to identify.

Production

Getting students to produce letters involves them in learning which direction the writing strokes go, and where to position the letters on lines. Once they are able to do this, they will then move on to writing cursively, forming 'joined-up' words:

tan ten tin tie time tall tell

'Joined-up' words from *Learn English Handwriting* by Bernard Hartley and Peter Viney

These examples practise lower-case letters, but the same techniques can be used with upper-case letters or a mixture of the two.

When students are confident about forming letters we can give them practice activities (which will also include a spelling element):

 The teacher dictates individual words. Students have to write them in their books or on the board.

The students have 3 columns. In the left column there is a list of words. The students read the left column. Then they cover it and write the words in the middle column. Then they compare what they have written with the left column, and, if necessary, write the word correctly in the right column.

Students are given an alphabetical list of animals. They have to write the words in one of three columns (headed 'pets', 'farm animals', and 'wild animals').

The teacher can ask questions (e.g. 'What's the first day of the week?' 'What pet starts with *c* and ends with *t*?' 'When does a new year start?') and the students have to write one-word answers.

All of the above activities are designed to give students practice in physically writing. Some of them rely on **copying** (see page 52).

The spelling challenge

Many people say that English spelling is irregular and therefore difficult, and they make a feature of the lack of spelling-sound correspondence which, although not unique, is a feature of English. They point out that the same sounds can be spelt differently, as in *threw* and *through* which both sound as /θruː/; and the same spelling can be pronounced differently, as in *threw* and *sew* /səʊ/ or *through* and *trough* /trɒf/ which are said with completely different vowel sounds.

English spelling is complex but it is not completely random and is, in fact, fairly regular; there are usually clear rules about when certain spellings are and are not acceptable. English spelling rules do often have exceptions but these usually only apply to a small number of individual words. A standard regularity such as the fact that *gh* at the end of words is silent, for example, is broken by words like *enough*; yet *enough* is only one of seven words that behave in such a way. In the same way many English language spellers know the rule '*i* before *e* except after *c*' to explain the spelling of *believe* vs. *conceive*, but there are exceptions to this familiar rule (e.g. *seize*, *weird*, *species*, *Neil*). However, it is worth remembering that exceptions which cause confusion are just that – exceptions.

Learners of English need to be aware about how we use different spellings to distinguish between **homophones** (words that sound the same but are spelt differently) such as *threw* and *through*. Pairs of words that sound identical – like *sun* and *son*, *sew* and *so*, *threw* and *through* – are immediately differentiated in writing. What can be seen as a disadvantage in terms of sound and spelling correspondence, in other words, is actually serving an important and useful purpose.

Spellings make English relatively easy to read. Word roots, for example, are always recognisable even when we add **affixes**: **prefixes** (like *un-*, *dis-*) or **suffixes** (like *-ist*, *-able*, and *-ed*). It is easy to perceive the connection between *sing* and *singing*, or between *art* and *artist*, or *rule* and *ruler*. And similarly, the function of affixes is reflected in their spelling. For example, the *-ist* and *-est* endings are pronounced the same (/ɪst/) in the words *artist* and *fastest*; it is the spelling that makes it clear that whereas the first ending denotes someone who does something (*art*) the second gives a one-syllable adjective its superlative form.

Teaching spelling The best way of helping students to learn how to spell is to have them read as much as possible. **Extensive reading** (reading longer texts, such as simplified readers, for pleasure) helps students to remember English spelling rules and their exceptions, although many students may need some encouragement to do this kind of reading.

However, as teachers we can be more proactive than this. We can raise the issue of sound and spelling correspondence, give students word formation exercises, get them to work out their own spelling rules, and use a number of other activities to both familiarise themselves with spelling patterns and also practise them. Here are some ideas:

 Students hear words and have to identify sounds made by common **digraphs** (pairs of letters commonly associated with one sound, e.g. *ck* pronounced /k/) and **trigraphs** (three letters usually pronounced the same way, e.g. *tch* pronounced as /tʃ/).

 Although reading aloud may have some disadvantages (without preparation students tend to read falteringly), nevertheless it can be very useful when the teacher takes students through a short text, getting them to listen to words and then repeat them correctly, and then coaching them in how to read the passage 'with feeling'. If the text has been chosen to demonstrate certain spellings (as well as being interesting in itself), it can focus the students' minds on how specific spellings sound or indeed on how specific sounds are spelt.

 Students can read and listen to a series of words which all share the same sound (e.g. *small, always, organised, four, sort,* and *more*) and then identify what the sound is (/ɔː/). They can go on to see if the sound is present or not in other similarly spelt words (e.g. *call, our, work, port*). Such an activity raises their awareness of the **convergence** and **divergence** of sounds and their spellings.

The same effect can be achieved by focusing on a particular letter rather than on a particular sound. Students can be asked to listen to a number of different words containing the same letter and they then have to say what the sound of the letter is in each case. If the letter in question is <u>a</u>, for example, students can say for each word they hear whether <u>a</u> sounds like the <u>a</u> in c<u>a</u>t, or in <u>a</u> *bottle*, or in m<u>a</u>ny, or in s<u>ay</u>, or whether it sounds like the <u>o</u> in <u>o</u>r. They then read sentences such as the following:

Tony loves pl<u>a</u>ying golf much more than other g<u>a</u>mes.
He thinks it's <u>a</u>bsolutely f<u>a</u>scin<u>a</u>ting.
He thought S<u>a</u>turday's g<u>a</u>me on TV was am<u>a</u>zing.
I thought it w<u>a</u>s rather boring when I s<u>a</u>w it.
When he starts, 'H<u>a</u>s <u>a</u>nybody seen th<u>a</u>t film about golf?',
   everybody begs him not to go on!

Same letter, different sounds

47

And they have to match up the underlined <u>a</u>s with the sounds they have studied. Obviously where a word has two examples of <u>a</u>, the word may match up with different sounds depending on which underlined <u>a</u> is being focused on.

 Students can be asked to work out a rule by looking at the spellings of pairs or groups of words. Rather than being told, for instance, how spelling operates when words change their grammatical form, they can be given an exercise like the following (designed for pre-intermediate students or above):

Look at the following verbs in the infinitive and with a verb ending. Can you say when the final letter of the verb is doubled (e.g. *pp*) and when it is not?

clap	clapping	limp	limping
commit	committed	pardon	pardoned
crawl	crawling	prefer	preferred
hint	hinted	run	running
hit	hitting	sin	sinned
howl	howled	sing	singing
knit	knitted	sit	sitting

Such an exercise demands concentration on the part of students, some of whom find this kind of puzzle-solving more agreeable (and easier) than others. We might note, too, that it only deals with three of the 'doubling' rules – because to do all of them in one go might be too much. Nevertheless it has the advantage of showing students, in unequivocal terms, that English spelling is not random.

 Many dictionary activities are suitable for not only training students in dictionary use, but also helping them to notice and absorb English spellings.

Asking lower intermediate students to put a written list of words in alphabetical order (and then to check against a dictionary) is useful in focusing the students' attention on the spelling of the initial letters of words. A variation for upper intermediate students or above which forces them to think about whole words is for the teacher to ask a question such as: 'How many words would you expect to find in a dictionary between *each* and *earphones*?' and then to say 'When you have listed as many as you can, check with your dictionary.'

 Dictation is an excellent technique for spelling practice, especially if the dictation contains words which exemplify certain spelling rules (and/or exceptions).

There are many alternatives to the traditional approach where the teacher reads a paragraph or two to the learners. Students can try to write the words they hear on a tape or they can dictate to each other. The technique known as running dictation (where individual students go to the front of the room one by one and read a line of a poem, say, which they then have to take back and dictate to their group) is ideal for spelling practice, especially if the teacher has said that each group will get points for the correct spelling of each and every word.

 At lower levels, students can be given cards with letters written on them and out of which they have to make words. The cards should not only have individual letters on them (e.g. *a*, *b*, *c*, etc.) but also digraphs, trigraphs, and vowel + consonant combinations, e.g.

Other games which can be used for spelling practice are:
- 'noughts and crosses' (or 'tic-tac-toe' as it is often called) where students have to pick letter clusters from one of the nine squares and make words with them. If they are successful, they can cover that square with a nought (0) or a cross (X) in order to try and make a three-square straight line.
- 'secret codes' where each letter is given a number (A = 1, B = 2, etc.) and students have to write messages to each other using numbers which the receiving student has to decode back into letters.
- 'backward spelling' where the teacher or students spell words backwards and then see who is the first person to guess the words.

Teaching punctuation

Using punctuation correctly is an important skill. Many people judge the quality of what is written not just on the content, the language, and the writer's handwriting but also on their use of punctuation. If capital letters, commas, full stops, sentence and paragraph boundaries, etc. are not used correctly, this can not only make a negative impression but can, of course, also make a text difficult to understand.

Where writers are using e-mail communication, the need for accurate punctuation (or spelling) does not seem to be so great. Features such as capital letters and apostrophes are frequently left out. However, even e-mails can sometimes be more formal or official and then such careless use of the computer keyboard may make a poor impression.

If we want our students to be good writers in English we need to teach them how to use punctuation conventions correctly (see Appendix A). This means teaching aspects of the system from the very beginning so that by the time they have reached upper intermediate level, students can do a revision exercise such as this one with ease:

C Check your punctuation

- Make sure you know the right punctuation symbols, and when to use them. Complete the rules with the right names.

**brackets   capital letters   colon   comma   full stop
hyphen   inverted commas   question mark
exclamation mark   apostrophe**

Symbol   Use

1 [.] A _____ shows the end of a sentence, and is also used after initials (P.J. Proby) and abbreviations (etc.).

2 [,] A _____ shows a short pause that separates parts of a sentence, e.g. a non-defining relative clause or words in a list.

3 ["] _____ show words that are spoken (direct speech). They are also used around titles of books or films, or a nickname.

4 [()] _____ show extra information or an explanation which is not considered essential.

5 ['] An _____ is used when two words are contracted, and to show possession, e.g. *It's Jane's.*

6 [-] A _____ is used when two words are joined together, e.g. some compound nouns.

7 [!] An _____ is used to show surprise. It comes at the end of a sentence and is often used in dialogue.

8 [?] A _____ (at the end of the sentence) shows that a direct question is being asked. It is also used in requests, e.g. *Could you bring me …?*

9 [:] A _____ tells you that something is coming next, for example a list.

10 [A B C] _____ are used for the first letter of a name, a country, nationality or language, days of the week, months.

From *English File: Upper Intermediate* by Clive Oxenden and Christina Latham-Koenig

Here are some ideas for getting students to recognise aspects of punctuation and be able to use them:

 Students at elementary level can study a collection of words and identify which ones are written with capital letters, e.g.

> Anita, and, apple, April, Argentina, art, Australian, Andrew, act, at, in, island, I, ice, Iceland

They then work out why some words have capital letters and some do not.

 Once students have had full stops, commas, and capital letters explained to them, they can be asked to punctuate a short text such as this:

> they arrived in cambridge at one o'clock in the morning it was cold with a bright moon making the river cam silver andrew ran to the water's edge angela hurrying to keep up with him ran straight into him by mistake and pushed him into the river

 Students can be shown a passage and asked to identify what punctuation is used and why. The following example for intermediate students shows a procedure for helping students to write direct reported speech.

The teacher gives the students an extract like this one (preferably from a book (reader) they are currently reading):

> 'I'm sorry to keep you waiting,' a voice said. The speaker was a short man with a smiling, round face and a beard. 'My name's Cabinda,' he said. 'Passport police.'
>
> 'I can explain,' Monika said quickly. 'My hair. It's not like the photograph. I know. I bought hair colour in South Africa. I can wash it and show you.'
>
> Cabinda looked carefully at Monika and then at the photo. 'No, that's OK. I can see that it's you,' Cabinda said. 'There's one more thing. You need a visa. It's ten dollars. You can pay the passport officer. Welcome to Mozambique!'

From *Double Cross* by Philip Prowse

Students are then asked to punctuate the following lines of dialogue in exactly the same way as the text (which they can refer to as they do the exercise):

> I'm sorry to keep you waiting a voice said My name's Cabinda he said Passport police
>
> I can explain Monika said quickly My hair It's not like the photograph I know I bought hair colour in South Africa I can wash it and show you
>
> No, that's OK I can see that it's you Cabinda said There's one more thing You need a visa It's ten dollars You can pay the passport officer Welcome to Mozambique

This activity asks them to look carefully at inverted commas, exclamation marks, commas, and full stops.

When they have completed the activity and the teacher has checked it through with them, they can be asked to answer the following questions:

> a) **How do we show that someone is speaking?**
> b) **When someone finishes speaking, where does the comma go – before or after the inverted comma (')?**
> c) **Where do we put the exclamation mark (!) – before or after the inverted comma (')?**

These three ways of dealing with punctuation (asking students to notice something, asking them to punctuate something, and, combining the two, asking them to explain how punctuation works) are highly effective activities. Teachers can also emphasise punctuation by saying that for a certain piece of homework they will only correct punctuation errors.

Copying The copying activities we have looked at so far in this chapter have involved copying single and 'joined-up' letters, copying words from a list, and rewriting words in different columns. The intention in each case was to have students learn how to form letters and words from a given model.

Quite apart from its potential for helping students to learn (as we have seen with handwriting and spelling), copying is an important skill in real life too. Some students, however, are not very good at it. In part this may be due to an inability to notice key features of English spelling or to a general difficulty with attention to detail. Matters are not helped by the computer: the ability to copy and paste chunks of text into any document means that there is no need to take account of the ways the words themselves are formed. Graeme Porte, who was working at the University of Granada in Spain, found that some of his 'underachieving' students had great difficulty copying accurately when making notes or when answering exam questions, for example. As a result he had these same students, under time pressure, copy a straightforward text which was set out in fairly short lines. They copied line by line, but at any one time they covered the whole text apart from the line they were working on. This meant that they could give their whole concentration to that one line. Their ability to copy accurately improved as a result of this activity.

Here are some other copying procedures designed both for learning spelling and for encouraging accurate copying itself:

 Disguised word copying – when students had to rewrite animal names in three different columns (see page 46) they were in effect engaged in a disguised form of word copying. There are many such activities. We may give students a list of words randomly organised which they then have to rewrite in alphabetical order. We may give students a list of words they have recently met and ask them to write down their five most favourite and five least favourite words from the list. We can also give them sentences which they have to write in appropriate boxes or columns, e.g.

Write the following sentences about mobile/cellular phones in the correct columns.

My phone makes me feel safe.
People are always 'somewhere else'.
People shout when they use them.
They are bad for your health.
They are very useful.
They're horrible.

Mobile phones are good	Mobile phones are bad

Students can also be asked to label plans, maps, tables, and graphs with a given list.

Of course many of these activities may have other uses (apart from just copying practice, that is), but if students are encouraged to concentrate on accurate copying this can only be helpful in fostering their attention to detail.

Copying from the board – teachers frequently get students to copy things from the board, whether what they copy is a word, a list of words, a diagram, a page number, a map, or an address. Very often, however, students do not copy accurately.

It is worth drawing students' attention to this by having occasional sessions in which copying from the board is turned into a game or task in its own right. The teacher can write up on the board words or phrases with potentially difficult spellings (*occur*, *necessary*, *commitment*, *desperate*, etc.). Students have exactly thirty seconds to look at the words before the teacher rubs them off the board and the students then have to try and write them correctly.

When students copy diagrams, addresses, etc. from the board they can hand what they have written to a fellow student so that each student's work can be checked by someone else.

 Making notes – there are many reasons why students have to take notes. Sometimes, as we shall see in Chapter 5, it is a way of generating ideas. Sometimes, as we shall see in Chapter 6, it is part of a longer 'process-writing' sequence. But because note taking involves copying, it is a useful activity for improving the skill itself. Teachers can get students to read encyclopaedia entries about a country and write down accurately as many place names as they can find. They can read a text about a figure from history and write down the names of the other people mentioned there. They can be sent to a computer screen – without being allowed to use a printer – and told to find out information on a certain topic, using only a pen and paper to collect as much information as they can.

In all these activities it will be useful for the teacher to check the notes to see if students have copied down information correctly. If they have not done so, the teacher can indicate where the problem is and then send the students back to the book or screen to correct their 'mis-copying'.

 Whisper writing – the spoken version of this game (often called 'Chinese whispers') involves students whispering a given sentence down a line. The game is to see whether the sentence which emerges at the end of the line is the same as the one that started the procedure. The written version of this game begins with a student at one end of the line being given a written sentence such as the following:

> Alistair McDonald lives in Wymondham.

The student is allowed only half a minute or so to read the sentence but is told that the spelling really matters. The sentence is then taken away and the student has to write their version of it from memory. They then show what they have written to the next student in the line who has only a short time to read it before the sentence is taken away. The second student now writes their version and repeats the procedure with the third student, and so on. The last student writes the sentence on the board. The teacher then writes up the original sentence.

In order to stop students getting bored either before or after they have written their version of the sentence, this game might be played while they are involved in some other task, or two sentences might be started from either end of the line. But at the very least whisper writing demonstrates the difficulty and desirability of accurate copying.

Sentence, paragraph, and text

Students need to learn and practise the art of putting words together in well-formed sentences, paragraphs, and texts. One way of doing this is parallel writing where students follow a written model, as the following examples will show:

Sentence production (elementary)
The most basic form of parallel writing is the kind of sentence writing that is often used for grammar reinforcement. Students are given one or two model sentences and then have to write similar sentences based on information they are given or on their own thoughts.

In this lesson example, students are given information about a particular character. They then see how this information can be combined in sentences with *and* and *but*. They have to write similar sentences about themselves.

Look at the following information about Carlos' likes (✓) and dislikes (✗) and read the sentences which follow.

Carlos   *Music:* hip hop (✓), classical music (✗)
           Sport: football (✓), tennis (✓)
           Entertainment: films (✓), clubs (✓)
           Food: spicy food (✓), raw fish (✗)

He likes hip hop but he doesn't like classical music.
He likes football and tennis.
He likes watching films and going out to clubs.
He likes spicy food but he doesn't like raw fish.

Now write similar sentences saying what music, sport, entertainment, and food you like. Use *and* and *but*.

Paired sentences (intermediate)
The following example asks students to look at how pronouns are used in a text and then gets them to write pairs of sentences in which they

use pronouns in the same way based on information they are given. Students read the following story:

On the second of January 2003 Andrew Cooney became the youngest person ever to walk to the South Pole. He is a 23-year-old scout leader. He telephoned his parents in Britain at 7.59 p.m. to say that he had completed the journey. It took two months.

'We were delighted,' said his father Terry. 'We're very proud of him.' His mother Marilyn said that she was looking forward to him coming home.

Mr Cooney relied on his parents at home. 'They were great,' he told his brother Ian. 'I owe everything to them.'

They are then asked to say who or what the words *he, his, it, we, she, him,* and *they* refer to in the text, and how they know. They discuss the role of pronouns and possessives in avoiding repetition and in creating cohesion. They then complete the following exercise:

Read the notes about round-the-world yachtswoman Ellen MacArthur and write pairs of sentences for the two ideas in each bullet point. The second sentence should start with *she, her, he, his, it, they.*

- Saved school dinner money for three years to buy small boat – an eight-foot dinghy
- In 1994 Ellen sailed alone around Britain – 18 years old
- Trained with leading chronobiologist Claudio Stampi – now can sleep for as little as 20 minutes at a time to avoid being tired
- In 2000 was the youngest and fastest woman ever to complete the Vendée Globe solo round-the-world race – she was 24
- Ellen's boat was called Kingfisher – Kingfisher normally has a crew of 11 people, not one
- 35,000 people watched Ellen cross the finish line in Western France – cheered when she arrived
- Ellen's parents (Ken & Avril) are teachers in Derbyshire, England (there is no sea there) – very proud of their daughter
- Ellen's parents and younger brother Fergus, 19, were at the finishing line in France to greet her – Ellen's father got on board Kingfisher to embrace his daughter

> **Examples:** *Ellen MacArthur saved her dinner money to buy a boat. It was an 8-foot dinghy.*
> *In 1994 she sailed around Britain. She was only 18 years old.*

Students can then go on to write a paragraph or short text about Ellen MacArthur, using the 'Andrew Cooney' text as a model.

 Paragraph construction (elementary)

This example employs a 'substitution-drill' style of procedure to encourage students to write a paragraph which is almost identical to one they have just read. This is like a substitution drill in that new vocabulary is used within a set pattern or patterns. Students read the following paragraph:

> William Shakespeare is England's most famous playwright. He was born in Stratford-on-Avon in 1564, but lived a lot of his life in London. He wrote 37 plays including *Hamlet, Romeo and Juliet, Henry V,* and *Twelfth Night.* He died in Stratford-on-Avon in 1616.

After the teacher has made sure they have understood the information about Shakespeare, students are given the following table of information and asked to write a similar paragraph about Jane Austen:

Name:	Jane Austen
Occupation:	one of England's most famous writers
Date of birth:	1775
Place of birth:	Steventon, Hampshire
Lived:	Bath and Southampton (cities in the south of the UK)
Examples of work:	six novels, including *Emma* and *Mansfield Park*
Died:	1817, Winchester

Controlled text construction (intermediate)

The logical organisation of ideas (coherence) applies not just to paragraphs but to whole texts as well. In this example the students focus on the genre of 'report writing'. In Activity 1 they work out the appropriate sequence for a report's five elements. This raises their awareness about a typical organisation for such a report. In Activity 2 they look at a particular language issue (linking words) before moving on to Stages 1–3 to write a similar report to the one they first put in sequence.

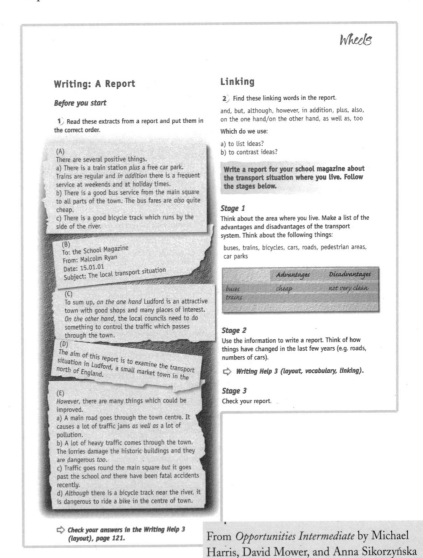

Wheels

Writing: A Report

Before you start

1 Read these extracts from a report and put them in the correct order.

(A)
There are several positive things.
a) There is a train station *plus* a free car park. Trains are regular and *in addition* there is a frequent service at weekends and at holiday times.
b) There is a good bus service from the main square to all parts of the town. The bus fares are *also* quite cheap.
c) There is a good bicycle track which runs by the side of the river.

(B)
To: the School Magazine
From: Malcolm Ryan
Date: 15.01.01
Subject: The local transport situation

(C)
To sum up, *on the one hand* Ludford is an attractive town with good shops and many places of interest. *On the other hand*, the local councils need to do something to control the traffic which passes through the town.

(D)
The aim of this report is to examine the transport situation in Ludford, a small market town in the north of England.

(E)
However, there are many things which could be improved.
a) A main road goes through the town centre. It causes a lot of traffic jams *as well as* a lot of pollution.
b) A lot of heavy traffic comes through the town. The lorries damage the historic buildings and they are dangerous *too*.
c) Traffic goes round the main square *but* it goes past the school *and* there have been fatal accidents recently.
d) *Although* there is a bicycle track near the river, it is dangerous to ride a bike in the centre of town.

⇨ *Check your answers in the Writing Help 3 (layout), page 121.*

Linking

2 Find these linking words in the report.

and, but, although, however, in addition, plus, also, on the one hand/on the other hand, as well as, too

Which do we use:

a) to list ideas?
b) to contrast ideas?

Write a report for your school magazine about the transport situation where you live. Follow the stages below.

Stage 1
Think about the area where you live. Make a list of the advantages and disadvantages of the transport system. Think about the following things:

buses, trains, bicycles, cars, roads, pedestrian areas, car parks

	Advantages	Disadvantages
buses	cheap	not very clean
trains		

Stage 2
Use the information to write a report. Think of how things have changed in the last few years (e.g. roads, numbers of cars).

⇨ *Writing Help 3 (layout, vocabulary, linking).*

Stage 3
Check your report.

From *Opportunities Intermediate* by Michael Harris, David Mower, and Anna Sikorzyńska

Parallel writing, in this example, is the last stage in a sequence which aims to raise the students' awareness of how a particular text genre is constructed before going on to ask them to imitate it.

Free text construction (elementary)

This final example uses the technique of parallel writing but it leaves the students free to decide how closely they wish to follow the original model. Instead of being bound by the layout and construction of the original they use it as a springboard for their imagination.

Students first read the following story about Stig, a large Alsatian dog:

A lucky escape

Stig was a big Alsatian dog who was becoming a bit of a problem. He lived with the Svensson family in their eighth-floor flat in Malmo in Sweden, but he was growing too big for the flat. The Svenssons were also worried that Stig was a danger to their two-year-old daughter, Mariette.

Then one day something extraordinary happened. Leif Svensson walked into the bedroom and noticed that the window was open. To his horror he saw that Mariette was crawling along the narrow ledge outside and Stig the Alsatian was following her along the ledge, only centimetres away.

Leif shouted for his wife. When she arrived, Stig was next to Mariette. Leif and his wife were beginning to fear the worst when suddenly the dog took the little girl's trousers in his teeth and started to walk slowly backwards along the ledge. Stig carried the child back to the open window and Leif pulled them both inside.

'We can never repay Stig,' said Leif later. 'He saved Mariette's life. From now on we're going to feed him the best steak money can buy!'

After reading the story and answering questions about it (and discussing the story), students complete the following exercise:

Use the story of Stig the Alsatian to help you write a magazine article about an animal. Use your imagination or write a story which has been in the news recently.

Last winter a man and a woman were walking with their dog near a lake. It was very cold and there was ice on the lake. Suddenly the dog ran ...

Think about these questions.

- What kind of animal was it?
- Where did the story take place?
- Who were the people and what were they doing?
- What did the animal do?
- What reward did it get?

From *Snapshot Elementary* by Brian Abbs, Ingrid Freebairn, and Chris Barker

We are moving away from the tight control of much parallel writing; instead, the students are being asked to write more creatively. The material gives them some help by offering a possible story opening and pointing them towards the content of what they will write with some pertinent questions. The nuts and bolts of writing are largely taken for granted and the students are encouraged to complete a 'writing-for-writing' activity.

Conclusions   In this chapter we have:
- looked at the challenge that handwriting presents for some students and shown ways of helping them to improve in this area.
- discussed why spelling is a problem for many students.
- looked at the relationship between spelling and sounds, and between spelling and word formation (in the case of word roots and affixation).
- shown a number of examples of activities to teach spelling.
- shown activities to help students to use English punctuation correctly.
- discussed why and how copying should be used in the teaching of writing.
- looked at various examples of parallel writing which can help students to learn the nuts and bolts of various aspects of writing.

Looking ahead
- In the next chapter we will look at ways of getting students to feel comfortable with writing and to feel enthusiastic about it.
- In Chapter 6 we will concentrate on lesson sequences which demonstrate the pedagogic value of both process writing and genre-based text construction.
- In Chapter 7 we will consider how best to respond to student writing, and in Chapter 8 we will consider how journal writing can benefit both students and teachers.

5 Building the writing habit

'Begin at the beginning,' the King said, very gravely, 'and go on till you come to the end: then stop.'
from 'Alice's Adventures in Wonderland' by Lewis Carroll

- Building confidence and enthusiasm
- Instant writing
- Collaborative writing
- Writing to each other
- What to do with 'habit-building' writing

Building confidence and enthusiasm

Although some students are always happy to have a go at writing in English, others can be less keen. This unwillingness may derive from anxieties they have about their handwriting, their spelling, or their ability to construct sentences and paragraphs. And if these insecurities are reinforced because they are unable to complete writing tasks successfully, then the students' attitude to writing is likely to become more and more negative.

The students' reluctance to write can also be because they rarely write even in their own language, and so the activity feels alien. Another powerful disincentive is the fear that they have 'nothing to say' – a common response of many students when asked to write. Finally, writing just does not interest some students; such people seem to be unwilling to invest the time and effort that they think a writing task demands.

With students like this who lack familiarity or confidence with writing (or indeed enthusiasm for it) we need to spend some time building the **writing habit** – that is making students feel comfortable as writers in English and so gaining their willing participation in more creative or extended activities. This will involve choosing the right kinds of activity – with appropriate levels of challenge – and providing them with enough language and information to allow them to complete writing tasks successfully.

Choosing writing tasks and activities

It is important that we choose writing activities which have a chance of appealing to our students – and which have, if possible, some relevance for them. Writing fairy stories might appeal to children but could fail to inspire a group of university students (though that is not necessarily the case, of course, as we shall see on page 79).

If we are lucky we will have a good idea of not only what kind of writing students are likely to have to do in English in the future, but also what kind of subjects and tasks they will enjoy – or have enjoyed in the past. This will help us choose writing tasks either because students need them or because they are likely to be motivated by them because the tasks are engaging in themselves.

An **engaging** writing task is one that involves students not just intellectually but emotionally as well; it amuses them, intrigues them, or makes them feel good. When students are 'switched on' by engaging tasks there is a good chance that some of their doubts about writing will disappear.

What engages people may be different for different students, but clearly the stimulus we provide (to encourage them to write) will make a difference. Music, for example, can be used to awaken the students' creativity, especially if they respond particularly well to **auditory** input. Pictures can have the same effect for those who are stimulated by **visual** input. Having students write jointly on the board or swap papers around caters for those who respond to **kinaesthetic** stimulation (to movement and physical activity). Writing tasks can be initiated and conducted in a number of different ways, in other words, and if we are to build the writing habit in the greatest number of our students we need to be aware of the variety of tastes and interests they have.

Except in the most goal-focused ESP classes, students are likely to respond best to a wide variety of tasks, topics, and genres over a period of time. Though we may want to revisit a writing genre – so that students can apply what they learned first time round for this second try – we will want to give students the widest range possible. Variety is as important in writing tasks and the activities that go with them as it is for other areas of language learning such as speaking, listening, and reading.

What students need

As we saw at the beginning of this chapter, there are many reasons why students may not be confident or willing writers. In order to counteract these potential problems we have to identify what our students need if they are to have a reasonable chance of success:

- **Information & task information** – students need to have the necessary information to complete the task. This means that they need to understand clearly what we want them to do and they need, also, to be absolutely clear about any of the topic detail that we give them. If we ask them to respond to an invitation, for example (see page 36), they need to have understood the details of the invitation, who they are writing to, and what it is they are trying to achieve. If we ask them to write a poem, they need to have a clear understanding of the topic(s) they will be dealing with. If they are involved in a collaborative writing activity they need to know what they are writing about, who writes what, and how the writing sequence is going to progress.

- **Language** – if students need specific language to complete a writing task we need to give it to them (or help them to find it). This may involve offering them phrases, parts of sentences, or words.

  Of course there are times when we just get students to write 'without thinking', to provoke their use of all and any of the language they know. But where a task depends on certain written formulae it would be pointless not to offer these to the students.

- **Ideas** – teachers need to be able to suggest ideas to help students when they get stuck. For some this may be just a word or two. For others we may need to dictate a half sentence or even something more substantial. One of the skills of a good writing teacher is to be able to throw out suggestions without crowding out the individual students with too much oppressive detail. In order to do this we have to be aware of which students need more or less help and stimulation, especially where students are working on their own rather than collaboratively (see below).

- **Patterns & schemes** – one way of helping students to write, even when they may think they do not have many ideas, is to give them a pattern or a scheme to follow. In 'worked-on' writing this will frequently happen when students first study a writing genre and then create their examples of the same genre (e.g. 'an advertisement', 'a postcard', 'a curriculum vitae', etc.). Even with more instant writing, however, the students' lives will be made much easier if there is a pattern or scheme to follow. The poetry activities we will look at in this chapter bear this out, as do some of the collaborative writing procedures. In these cases students are given a frame to write in and, while this may make the task less creatively free, it does offer the writers support. It is often easier to write when constrained than it is when there is nothing in front of you except for a blank piece of paper or a blank screen.

When students are involved in the kind of process writing or genre-based construction we talked about in the first two chapters of this book, the identification of suitable topics and tasks and an analysis of what they need to complete the tasks successfully are both absolutely vital. They are important, too, for tasks which aim to build the writing habit – that is tasks whose principal aim is to have students writing fluently and enthusiastically, often with more spontaneity and less actual preparation than in process and genre approaches. Two such areas of habit building are **instant writing** and **collaborative writing**.

Instant writing

There are stages in any lesson where students can be asked to write on the spot, without much in the way of preparation or warning; this is **instant writing**.

Because instant writing is not part of a long writing process, it can be used whenever the teacher feels it is appropriate. The tasks may each take only ten or fifteen minutes or be even shorter; but a regular diet of such tasks will boost students' confidence, if they are appropriate, since each time they will have something worthwhile and interesting to show for their efforts.

The following activities provide some examples of instant writing.

Sentence writing

As we have seen, students can be asked to write sentences either as language reinforcement or in preparation for a forthcoming activity. The following activities could also be used for such purposes, but their purpose here is to make reluctant writers feel more comfortable and to remove the problems of those who think they have nothing to say:

 Dictating sentences for completion – a very simple way of getting students to write creatively is to dictate part of a sentence which they then have to complete about themselves. For example, we can dictate the following:

'My favourite time of day is ...'

And students have to write *the morning*, or *the evening*, etc. This can be extended of course. The teacher can say: 'Now write one sentence saying *why* you have chosen your time of day.'

Just about any incomplete sentence can be used in this way, as the following examples demonstrate:

'The one thing I would most like to learn is how to ...'
'The best film I have ever seen is ...'
'One of the most exciting things that has ever happened to me is ...'

Teachers can also dictate sentence frames (or write them up on the board). If the topic is 'animals', we can say:

'Although I like ..., I'm not very keen on ...'

 Writing sentences – students can be asked to write two or three sentences about a certain topic. For example, suppose students have been working on the topic of 'hopes and ambitions', they can write three sentences about how they would like their lives to change in the future. If they are discussing education, they can write sentences about why exams are a good thing or a bad thing. If they have been discussing anti-social behaviour, the teacher can ask them to write three *don't* sentences (e.g. *Don't listen to loud music after eleven o'clock*).

 The weather forecast – at the beginning of the day the teacher asks students to write about themselves and their day as if they were writing a weather forecast: 'What's the "weather" like now? Are you happy or tired, listless or energetic? How are you likely to feel later on, in the afternoon?'

Activities like this work extremely well for some students, because they allow them to be creative in an amusing and thought-provoking way.

Sentence writing is one way of getting students to write quickly while at the same time allowing them to write things that mean something to them personally.

Using music

Music can be a very effective way to stimulate a writing activity since it often provokes strong feelings and ideas. There is a universality about music which means that much of it is easy for everyone to understand. You don't have to be a musical expert for a piece of music to make you feel happy, or sad, or wistful.

Choosing the right music is vitally important. Much of the best music (for writing purposes) is instrumental. We don't want students to be distracted by listening out for words. On the contrary, we want the music to speak to them directly. We need music they can respond to. A lot of classical music from around the world is very descriptive both in terms of mood and also because composers, both past and present, have tried to describe events and people with their compositions.

Among the many ways music can be used to stimulate instant writing are the following:

 Words – one activity is to play a piece of music and have students write down any words that come into their heads as they listen. Any emotive piece of music will do for this, such as – in the Western classical tradition – *Mars: the god of war* from Holst's *The Planets*, Barber's *Adagio for Strings*. We can also use music from films such as that in *The Piano* by Michael Nyman, in *The Mission* by Ennio Morricone, or just about anything by John Williams.

When students have written down the words which the music has suggested to them, they can share their words with the rest of the class to see how others have reacted.

 What is the composer describing? – a lot of music is written to describe particular scenes or places. The piece *Vltava* by the Czech composer Smetana describes a river. Rachmaninov's *Isle of the Dead* describes a bleak and desolate island. Vivaldi famously describes the seasons. Maxwell Davies in his piece *Highland Wedding* describes a drunken party with a dawn hangover. The music in *The Lord of the Rings* by Howard Shore is highly descriptive.

Students are told that in the piece – or pieces – of music they are about to hear the composer is trying to describe something specific. As they listen to the music they should write down whatever they 'hear' in the music.

When they have finished they can read out what they have written (or show it to their classmates). The teacher can then say what the music was intended to describe.

This activity can be made more specific by the teacher asking for example: 'What animal is the music describing?' (Saint-Saëns' *Carnival of the Animals* is useful for this.) 'What kind of a person is the composer writing about?' (e.g. Juliet in Prokofiev's *Romeo and Juliet*).

'How do you think the composer was feeling when he or she was composing this?' (The last movement of Tchaikovsky's *Pathétique* symphony is useful for this.)

 Film scores – in this activity students listen to a piece of music and then create the opening scenes for a film that the music suggests to them – they should describe the scenes before the dialogue starts. They can write in note form if they wish.

Film music can be used for this, but so too can any piece of evocative music such as the third movement from Debussy's string quartet, slow saxophone music, solo violin or cello music by Bach, or rock, trance, or folk music, for example.

Once again, when students have written the scene they imagined, they can compare what they have written with their classmates.

 How does it make me feel? – teachers can play students musical excerpts and get them to write their reactions as they listen. They can be given prompts which will help them to do this, such as: 'What colour do you think the music is?' 'Where would you most like to hear it, and who would you like to have with you when you do?'

 Musical stories – students can write stories on the basis of music they listen to. If the music conveys a strong atmosphere it will often spark the students' creativity and almost 'tell' them what to write.

One way of showing students this in an amusing way is for the teacher to dictate the first line of a story (e.g. *He turned and looked at her*). Students are told that they should continue the story when the music starts. 'The music will tell you what to write.' Students then hear a piece of music which is particularly nostalgic, or sad, or frenetic, for example.

The teacher tells students to turn their pieces of paper over and then dictates the same sentence again. Once again students are told to write the story based on some music, but this time a contrasting piece of music is played.

When all students have written their two stories, they show them to colleagues who then read out one of the stories. The class have to decide which bit of music it was written to.

Teachers should use musical activities sparingly, for two reasons. First, the activities mentioned here work best when they are unusual – something which gives them their special quality and which, as a result, allows them to provoke students' creativity. Second, not all students can respond immediately to music.

We need to be careful, also, not to play too long a piece of music. Students may well get something out of an excerpt which lasts for between two and three minutes but they may well lose interest in an excerpt which goes on for much longer than that.

Using pictures

Just as music can provoke creativity in students – especially those who are particularly responsive to auditory stimuli – so too pictures work really well as spurs to written production.

Pictures are often used to present situations for grammar and vocabulary work. But their ability to transport students to different worlds means that they can also be used to incite students to creative flights of fancy. As with music, you don't need to speak the language of pictures in order to be stimulated by them.

Among the many ways of using pictures for writing are the following:

 Describing pictures – one way of getting students to write about pictures is simply to ask them to write a description of one. If you give them a complex picture and a time limit, they have to write quickly to get down as much information as they can.

We can make the activity more engaging by asking students to write a description for someone who is unable to see the picture, either because they cannot get to see it or, perhaps, because they are blind.

When getting students to describe pictures we need to be sure they have the vocabulary necessary for the task.

Suspects and objects – a variation on picture description is to give students a variety of pictures and ask them to write about only one of them. Students could be shown the pictures of the people below, for example, and they have to write a description of one of them:

Suspect parade

When they have written their descriptions, the pictures are put up on the board. The students then give their description to another student who has to identify which picture is being described and, perhaps, stick the description under the correct picture.

67

The same activity can be used with any pictures or photographs that are similar to each other. Students can write descriptions of (pictures of) recovered stolen objects, for example. The class has to match the descriptions with the objects.

 Write the postcard – we can give students postcard scenes and then ask them to write the postcard which they would expect to write to an English-speaking friend from such a location.

Any holiday picture can be used for this activity. For example, we might show students photos of people in holiday locations and then ask them to write the postcard which those people would write.

 Portraits – whether students are actually looking at portraits in a gallery or see reproductions of them in a book or on the Internet, these can be used for a number of stimulating writing tasks. Students can write a letter to a portrait, asking the character questions about his or her life and explaining why they are writing to them. Here are two portraits (from the eighteenth and twenty-first centuries) which can be used in this way:

The teacher will tell the students to study the portrait and think about the person they see there. Do they look happy or sad, extrovert or introvert? When they have studied the portrait they will know what kind of letter they want to write.

Other students can write back as if they were the character. As with the original letter, they can get the clues they need by studying the subject's face, expression, clothes, and any actions they are doing.

We can also ask students to write a 'day in the life' diary of one of the characters. They can imagine what someone who looks like that does for a living and how they might spend their day.

These activities can be done with photographs too, of course, provided that they go some way to capturing the personality of the subject in the same way that good painted portraits do.

 Story tasks – pictures are really useful ways to prompt students into writing stories. There are a number of different tasks which students can be asked to undertake. Four which work well are the following:

- for dramatic pictures (such as a man crossing a canyon on a tightrope, people in a street protest, or someone who has come face-to-face with a wild animal) students can be asked to write what happened next.
- students can be given a series of pictures of random objects (an aeroplane, a bicycle, a pack of cards, a dog, a fireplace, etc.) and told to choose four of them, and write a story which connects them.
- students can be given a series of pictures in sequence which tell a story. They have to write the story which the pictures tell.
- students can be given a picture and a headline or caption and asked to write a story which makes sense of the picture and the words.

Writing poems

Many teachers have students write poems because 'poetry' allows students to express themselves in a way that no other genre does. Something really meaningful and powerful can be written in a much shorter space and time than a 'report', 'narrative', or 'essay' might take. Poetry writing also allows students to play with new vocabulary in a way that other genres do not.

Poetry-writing activities can be immensely satisfying for students precisely because they can express themselves at a much deeper level than in other writing activities, even where the poem is based on a pre-established pattern of some kind. Pre-established patterns are often necessary because without them some students will complain of having nothing to say or write. But just as with sentence-writing activities, the existence of a pattern gives them security within which to be creative.

The following activities show how pre-established patterns can be used to help students write poetry:

 Acrostic poems/alphabet poems – an acrostic poem is one where the first letters of each line, when read downwards, form a word, e.g.

> Blue sea, sunshine on waves
> Easy days
> Afternoons of heat and playfulness
> Charm of summer, anger of the storm
> Home, and the itch of sand

Students can be given any number of words to write acrostic poems for, such as *love*, *mother*, *school*, *football*, or *freedom*. If necessary the teacher can further circumscribe the activity by asking for the same grammatical pattern to be followed each time, e.g. adjective + noun.

The same technique can be applied to the alphabet with just about any topic. At low levels, students might just be asked to come up with one word for each letter. The topic could be anything from 'animals', 'things in the house', or 'people I admire', as here:

Actors
Business women
Chemists

etc.

At higher levels, students could be asked to write a 'my favourite things' alphabet poem with the pattern *A is for ... that ...*, like this one:

A is for armchairs that make me comfortable
B is for butter that I spread on my bread
C is for children that laugh

etc.

Other 'list'-type poems include giving students a list of colours and they then have to write sentences like *Red is the sun sinking, Blue is the morning sea ... .*

Although such student productions are unlikely to achieve the status of high art, nevertheless, they allow students to use language in a playful and different way.

 Stem/frame poems – many teachers give students sentence or phrase stems or frames for them to complete and which, when completed, make something that is almost a poem. We can give students a frame like this:

I like .... because ....
I like .... because ....
I like .... because ....
But I hate .... because ....

Students choose a topic, say 'fruit', and then have to complete the stems to make something like this:

> I like apples because they keep the doctor away.
> I like oranges because they taste fresh.
> I like pineapples because they look interesting.
> But I hate bananas because they're yellow.

Other stems might be *I think, I believe, I wish, I hope*, or indeed anything that will encourage students to express their thoughts and feelings.

 Metaphor generators – one of the reasons why poems are attractive to students is that they allow them to write about things using metaphor – instead of always having to describe things literally. However, using language metaphorically in English is a significant challenge for any student whether or not they are native speakers.

Some time ago a series of poetry workshops with 9–11 year olds in a Cambridge primary school produced poetry such as the following:

> To Philip
>
> You are creamy garlic cheese
> Wind as it rushes in the trees.
> You are an untidy desk with paper spilling on the floor
> A friendly train, old and dirty
> Boots in a shade of green, torn at the edges.
> You're a door that needs oiling
> In a musty shade of blue.
> You are home-baked bread
> A long haired monkey swinging in the trees
> An October morning when grass is crisp.
>
> Tanya (aged 9)
>
> From *Poets Live in Cambridge* edited by H Cook and Y Bradbury

This poem was produced in line with specific instructions. The children were first asked to think of someone they loved/liked and to write that person's name at the top of the page. They were then told to start the first line with the word *You* and write about their person as if they were a kind of food (hence the line *You are creamy garlic cheese*). Next they had to write about the person as if they were a kind of weather. In subsequent lines participants had to write about their person as if they were a kind of furniture, a kind of transport, a kind of clothing, etc.

The point about this kind of activity is that students end up with something which can often be extremely meaningful. By being given a framework for the poem, it is probable that they will be able to produce such poems fairly quickly, and then exhibit their work both for their own pleasure and that of their classmates and the people they have written about.

Although the activity being described here was used with primary school students, it can be used with students of all ages and all levels to great effect.

 Model poems – in her book *Writing*, Tricia Hedge describes how young Chinese poets frequently chose to emulate their elders by writing about the same themes and/or using the same poetic forms. Writers have always imitated and borrowed from each other, of course, and our students can do the same if we or they can find an appropriate poem for them to work with. Roger McGough's poem *In two minds* – although only suitable for relatively advanced students – provides an example of such a model:

> In two minds
>
> What I love about night
> is the silent certainty of its stars
> What I hate about stars
> is the overwhelming swank of their names
> What I love about names
> is that every complete stranger has one
> What I hate about one
> is the numerical power it holds over its followers
> What I love about followers
> is the unseemly jostle to fill the footsteps
> What I hate about footsteps
> is the way they gang up in the darkness
> What I love about darkness
> is the soft sighing of its secrets
> What I hate about secrets
> is the excitement they pack into their short lives
> What I love about lives
> is the variety cut from the same pattern
> What I hate about pattern
> is its dull insistence on conformity
> What I love about conformity
> is the seed of rebelliousness within
> What I hate about within
> is the absence of landscape, the feel of the weather
> What I love about the weather
> is its refusal to stay in at night
> What I hate about night
> is the silver certainty of its stars
>
> From *Everyday Eclipses* by Roger McGough

Because this poem follows a rigorous scheme (the alternation of *love* and *hate*, the last word of each couplet becoming the topic of the next, and the last topic being the same as the first but after *hate* rather than *love*), students quickly pick up the design when you first read them this poem. Although they may not understand all the phrases (*overwhelming swank of their names*), they soon know which verb is coming next and what will follow *love about …* or *hate about …* . They can then write their own versions on any topic they choose following the same basic scheme.

All the poetry activities in this section have been designed for fairly instant writing. The students quickly understand a model and then follow it by producing similarly formed writing of their own. Poetry does not have to be this 'formulaic', however, and in Chapter 6 we will be looking at longer poetry-writing sequences which offer students greater freedom for creativity.

Collaborative writing

The car designer Sir Alec Issigonis is credited as the originator of the phrase 'a camel is a horse designed by a committee', and it may well be that in the world of design too many people do, indeed, get in the way of sensible decision making. Yet group activities in a language classroom have a very different flavour. Successful collaborative writing allows students to learn from each other. It gives each member of the collaboration access to others' minds and knowledge, and it imbues the task with a sense of shared goals which can be very motivating. And in the end, although the collaborators may have to share whatever glory is going (rather than keep it for themselves individually), still, any less-than-successful outcome is also shared so that individuals are not held solely responsible for any shortcomings in what they produce. For these reasons **collaborative writing**, as exemplified in the following activities, has the power to foster the writing habit in a unique way.

Using the board

One way of making collaborative writing successful is to have students write on the board. This gets them out of their chairs; it is especially appropriate for those who respond well to kinaesthetic stimuli. It also allows everyone to see what is going on. Two activities show how the board can be used in this way:

 Sentence by sentence – in the activity on page 37 we saw how students built up a letter in reply to an invitation on the board, sentence by sentence. Each time a new student goes up to the board in such activities, the rest of the class (or the group that student represents) can help by offering suggestions, corrections, or alternatives.

This kind of writing activity has the great advantage of creating a clear focus for everyone in the room, and can create a feeling of shared achievement.

Dictogloss – in his book *How to Teach Grammar*, Scott Thornbury describes a procedure called **dictogloss**, in which students re-create a text or story that the teacher reads to them. One purpose of the activity is to focus the students' attention on specific items of language by getting them to analyse the difference between their written re-creations and the original which they have heard.

Dictogloss is useful for vocabulary acquisition too in very much the same way. And on top of that it is especially appropriate for building the writing habit.

In the following example the teacher uses their own words to tell students the story of a boy called Jesse Arbogast who was attacked by a shark. The first time they hear the story students are told just to listen and not to make notes. The teacher uses whatever language, mime, or gesture necessary to ensure that the students understand the main facts of the story.

In pairs, the students now discuss what they have heard and try to establish the main facts of the story. Once this has been done the teacher tells them that they are going to hear the story again, and that this time they should make notes – although they are advised not to try and write down too much. Now they will be able to concentrate not only on the facts, but also the language. This is what the students hear:

How Jesse got his arm back

Eight-year-old Jesse Arbogast was playing in the sea late one evening in July 2001 when a 7-foot bull shark attacked him and tore off his arm. Jesse's uncle leapt into the sea and dragged the boy to shore. The boy was not breathing. His aunt gave him mouth-to-mouth resuscitation while his uncle rang the emergency services. Pretty soon, a helicopter arrived and flew the boy to hospital. It was a much quicker journey than the journey by road.

Jesse's uncle, Vance Folsenzier, ran back into the sea and found the shark that had attacked his nephew. He picked the shark up and threw it onto the beach. A ranger shot the fish four times and although this did not kill it, the shark's jaws relaxed so that they could open them, and reach down into its stomach, and pull out the boy's arm.

At the Baptist Hospital in Pensacola a plastic surgeon, Dr Ian Rogers, spent eleven hours reattaching Jesse's arm. 'It was a complicated operation,' he said, 'but we were lucky. If the arm hadn't been recovered in time, we wouldn't have been able to do the operation at all. What I mean is that if they hadn't found the shark, well then we wouldn't have had a chance.'

According to local park ranger Jack Tomosvic, shark attacks are not that common. 'Jesse was just unlucky,' he says, 'evening is the shark's feeding time. And Jesse wasn't in a lifeguard area. This would never have happened if he had been in a designated swimming area.'

When reporters asked Jesse's uncle how he had had the courage to fight a shark, he replied, 'I was mad and you do some strange things when you're mad.'

Jesse's story

Students once more discuss in pairs what they have heard and then, for the last time, the teacher reads exactly the same text again, while the students make more notes.

The class is now divided, randomly, into groups of 3 or 4. Each group is given marker pens and rolls of paper. Their only task is to recreate the story in writing – as far as possible using the words and language they have heard. The only help the teacher needs to give them is to write some names (*Jesse Arbogast, Vance Folsenzier,* etc.) up on the board.

When the groups have finished, their versions can be stuck up on the board or the walls. Here are two versions that were written by students (in a significantly mixed ability group) doing this activity:

How Jesse got his arm back

There was an 8-year boy named Jesse Arbogast. In July 2001, he was playing on the beach with his uncle's family in Florida. He paddled in the sea, suddenly the shark ~~attacked~~ attacked him and ~~took~~ tore off his arm.

His uncle ~~draged~~ dragged him to the shore, meanwhile the boy ~~couldn't~~ was not breathing His ~~an~~ aunt gave him CPR, and called 911, Luckily, there ~~is~~ was a ~~hand~~ helicopter near ~~their are~~ this area. Before Jesse went to hospital, The ranger ha shot the shark and the mad uncle took the shark and p threw it on the beach, opened its mouth, reached ~~it~~ to the stomach, and took Jesse's arm.

The helicopter took them to the Pensacda Hospital. There ~~were~~ was an 11 hours operation, they a reattched Jassis's arm, He was a very lucky boy.

According to the ~~a~~ local news "Jack Tomosvic" evening is shark's ~~e~~ feeding time, and the area where Jesse went is not designated swimming area. Jesse's uncle said "I was mad. When you were mad, you do strange things."

Students' versions of *Jesse's story*
Group A

How Jesse got his arm back

In July 2001 a boy named Jesse was attacked by a bull shark at the beach while he was paddling. The shark tore off his arm. When his uncle and aunt found him, he was not breathing at all. His aunt gave him the mouth-to-mouth resuscitation. Luckily, there was a helicopter hovering around, and it came along as soon as the crew heard the news. The boy was sent to the Pensacola Hospital right away. And his uncle was so mad that he went back to the beach and saw the shark that attacked his nephew, he picked it up and threw it onto the beach. The ranger came and shot the shark 4 times. And the shark's mouth was relaxed. They opened its mouth, ~~and~~ reached down the stomach and pull out the boy's arm. The plastic surgeon Ian Rogers, spent 11 hours reattaching his arm. The surgery was complicated but successful. The operation wouldn't have been successful if his arm hadn't been recovered in time. One of the local park rangers said, evening is the shark's feeding time, and Jesse wasn't at the designated swimming area at that time. His uncle said, "I was so mad. And you do strange things when you are mad."

Students' versions of *Jesse's story*
Group B

The students are then shown the original 'Jesse's story', which they had heard read to them, and are asked to amend what they have written.

In trying to write a text collaboratively the students have been provoked into using what they have heard, and any other language they know, to help write the story. At the end of the activity they have something to display and look at, they can compare different versions, and then they have an opportunity to compare what they have written with a correct version.

Writing in groups and pairs

There are many activities which are suitable for students writing in pairs and groups. Some of them depend on a **scribe** to write the final version of the piece, while some of them involve every single person writing their own version of the text.

The advantage of having a scribe is that the other students have more chance to concentrate on the language, think about what is being written, and evaluate it in a more objective way, perhaps, than they judge their own individual efforts. The disadvantages are that not everyone is getting actual writing practice, and the scribe may make little contribution to the construction of the text but rather act only as a secretary taking dictation. One way round these problems is for the teacher to make sure that different students take on the scribe role in the course of an activity. However, the main objective of writing activities done in groups or pairs is to involve everyone in the creation of written text, whoever does the actual writing.

Although all of these activities are suitable for use with paper and pen, they can also be done at a computer with students crowded around a screen. This can be particularly motivating, because correction can be instant through the use of a grammar and/or a spell-check and because any problems with hard-to-read handwriting are removed.

 Rewriting (and expanding) sentences – in one sentence-rewriting activity, students are presented with a stereotypical statement and asked to amend it to reflect the opinions of the group. This provokes discussion not only about the topic but also about how to write a consensus opinion appropriately.

The teacher (with the class) has chosen a topic for the students to consider. The students are then presented with some examples of stereotypical statements, like these on the topic of gender differences:

> Boys like football.
> Girls like shopping.

They have to rewrite the sentences so that they accurately reflect the views of the group. One group might think, for example, that while some boys are crazy about football others are considerably less interested. They might want to say that lots of girls like football as well, or that many boys feel pressured to like football even if, in reality, they are not that interested. Another sentence-rewriting activity is to take a sentence and put far more detail into it. For example, we can give students a short sentence like this:

> The woman saw the man.

The students then have to expand the sentence with as many words as possible, e.g.

> When the pale, red-headed woman, who had arrived not less than an hour earlier than the time they had agreed on the night before, saw the tall, bearded man leaning unhappily against a poster advertising a new perfume which had just been launched onto the market, she knew at once that …

But the final elongated sentences have to make sense and be reasonably natural. In other words, a list of ten adjectives before a noun is, except in highly exceptional circumstances, not natural English.

This activity can be made competitive by making the winning pair or group the one which produces the most words with the fewest mistakes.

The sentences which the students produce in both these activities will obviously depend upon the level they are writing at. But in both cases the mixture of discussion ('What do we think about the topic?' in the first activity; 'How can we add more words and clauses?' in the second) and written execution helps students build good writing habits.

First lines, last lines – just as pictures can be used to provoke story writing, so first and last lines of possible stories can also be used to get students' imaginations going.

Students can be given either the first line of a story (e.g. *When she looked out of the window she saw a red car parked across the street*) or the last line (e.g. *He told himself that he would never go to the cinema by himself again*). They then have to write a story to include one or the other. They discuss the situation in their pairs or groups and create a story which follows on from the first line or ends with the last line. A scribe writes the story they come up with.

This activity needn't be confined to lines, however. We can give students opening and closing paragraphs and ask them to write the middle portion of a story. We can tell a story up to a certain point and then have them develop the story from that point.

A common group-writing activity which has all the students writing at the same time is the **story circle**. This starts with all the students in a group sitting in a circle. Each student has a blank sheet of paper in front of them. The teacher dictates a sentence (for example, 'Once upon a time a beautiful princess lived in a castle by a river', if the teacher and students had been talking about fairy stories and legends). They all write it at the top of their piece of paper. Each student is told to write the next sentence of the story. Once this has been done, they all pass their piece of paper to the left and each student writes the next sentence of the story they now have in front of them (which is different from the one they started with). The papers are then passed one place to the left again. Each student writes the next sentence of the story in front of them.

This procedure continues until each student has their original piece of paper in front of them. They are then told to write the last line of the story.

Here is one such story produced by a group from a multilingual, lower intermediate class (the participating students were Chinese, Turkish, Mexican, Spanish, and Korean):

Once a upon a time a beautif prinsess ~~leavt~~ cess lived in a ~~eas~~ castle by a river.

She was very clever. She always read and studied.

However she hasn't seen the gergous nature around her, where she was living, she had an stemother that he hate her very much. She had a lovely dog, it's was very loyalty. One day, her stepmother bought a basket of red apples from the local market.

The stepmother putted poison in apples.

Her dog ~~seen~~ saw ~~of this the~~ what the stepmother do, ~~w~~ so, when the stepmother ~~give~~ gave the apple to her, her dog jumped and ~~eate~~ ate the apple. then, the dog ~~w~~ died.

Student-generated fairy story

This story is full of language mistakes (we will look at ways of using these mistakes on page 118 in Chapter 7) and as a story it has its limitations, as it was produced under considerable time pressure. But it made the rest of the class laugh when they heard it and, more importantly, it made writing enjoyable. Despite problems of expression, the participants had produced something in writing without much preparation and they had taken pleasure in doing it.

 Directions, rules, instructions – a really useful activity is to ask students to write 'instructional' text for others to follow. This could take the form of writing directions to a place (how to get to their school from the station or the airport, for example).

Students can be asked, in groups, to write the four (or five, or six) principal rules of a game they like and know how to play. They are told that the rules must be as clear as they can make them so that there is no uncertainty about what is meant (though asking people to provide a clear statement of the current off-side rule in football would provide a significant challenge to anyone however good their language was!).

Groups can be asked to write instructions for an activity (anything from a dance, to assembling a piece of furniture) or computer process (how to download a document, how to use a particular software program). If possible, other groups in the class then have to follow the instructions carefully to see if they work.

This kind of writing is clearly not suitable for beginners. However, at intermediate levels and above it forces students to think carefully about what to write and in what order. Teachers may want to offer appropriate vocabulary either before the activity starts or by going round the groups while they are writing.

Story reconstruction – we can enhance the value of the story activities which involve a sequence of pictures (described on page 69) by adding a jigsaw element. This means that each student is given a different piece of a 'jigsaw' and, by sharing what they have seen or heard, they have to reassemble the bits into a coherent whole.

A classic use of jigsaw techniques is the story reconstruction activity. Here students are divided into, say, four groups (A, B, C, and D). Each group is given one of this set of pictures which they have to talk about and memorise as many details of as possible:

The pictures are then taken away. Students are now regrouped so that each new group has a student from the original groups A, B, C, and D.

In their new groups students have to work out a sequence for the four pictures and then create a written text which tells the story of that sequence.

This activity works well. It provokes a lot of discussion which, in turn, gets students to write with enthusiasm.

It is worth pointing out that many of the earlier activities in this chapter could also be worked on collaboratively with all the advantages we have suggested for such an approach. Nevertheless we will not want all writing tasks to be collaborative. Individual students need individual space sometimes.

Writing to each other

A further way of provoking student engagement with writing is to get students to write to each other in class time. They can also correspond with people outside the class. Some writing, when done in this way, becomes genuinely communicative and has a real purpose – even if it only gets going when a teacher sets the process in motion.

At its most basic level, such writing involves students writing notes to each other. The teacher can ask individual students to write a question to another student in the class. This can be anything from *Where are you from?* to *What do you find most difficult about learning English?* The note is addressed to another student and the teacher delivers it.

Teachers have been using this kind of note-writing for years as a way of encouraging lower-level students to put words down on paper. But writing to each other can go a lot further than this.

 Pen pals, e-mails, and live chat – teachers have always encouraged students to correspond with pen pals from different towns or countries. This is significantly easier and more immediate with e-mail exchanges between 'key pals' or 'mouse pals'.

Some teachers get in touch with classes from a school in a different country and, with their foreign colleagues, instigate initial exchanges to get the ball rolling. Teachers in Japan, for example, might get their English students to communicate with students of English in Colombia. They could start the process by getting their students to think of five questions about Colombia (maybe addressing stereotypes) that they would like to know the answers to. The Colombian students could do the same with questions about Japan. Alternatively, they could write e-mails about their lives or their families to start with.

Setting up a 'key pal' exchange system does not guarantee its success. Whereas one or two students may really get the bug and continue to mail their opposite numbers, others will get bored by the whole thing – unless, that is, the teacher monitors the procedure and helps with suggestions, comments, and encouragement.

The 'key pal' system does need computer access, of course. But if necessary we can still simulate e-mail exchanges on paper, using the same basic technique as the exchange of notes that we started this section with. On page 82 there is an example of a simulated e-mail exchange (between two intermediate students) using a form developed by the teacher John Hughes.

As with the fairy story earlier, the English in the simulated e-mails may not be especially correct, but the students participated with enthusiasm and found writing a congenial activity.

E-mail dialogue sheet

TO: Lin

FROM: Carolina

SUBJECT: Weekend plans

Hi Lin! How R U ? I hope good. I write you because me and my friends are going to london this saturday to see a play, come with us if you want,

answer me. see you then.

wbw Carolina.

TO: Carolina

FROM: Lin

SUBJECT: The time of play

Hi Carolina,
I'm fine. I like to attend your inviting but can you tell me the time of this play. I can arrange my schedule.
Bye
Lin

TO: Lin

FROM: Carolina

SUBJECT: Time play

Lin, there are two funcions if we want to see "lion king" it's at 3 o'clock, and if we wnat to see "mama mia" it's at 4 o'clock.

please tell me which one you like to see. I wait for your answer. Bye, Cas

TO: Carolina

FROM: Lin

SUBJECT: where and when we meet

Carolina,
The time of "lion king" is suited for my schedule.
Where and when will we meet?
Lin

A simulated e-mail exchange between intermediate students

A logical extension of e-mail exchanges is the live chat environment, where students are talking to each other in real time and writing becomes more and more like a conversation. Here students may well be extremely motivated to key in their contributions. There is still something exciting about being in communication with people who are any number of miles away. The fact that words appear on the screen (which all participants can see) lends this activity an immediate excitement that even a two-way phone call may not have.

Ken Hyland quotes an example of two Hong Kong students chatting online; here is an example of their interactions:

> **Jj:** hi, i just go and check e-mail and after that i will go to sleep, how about u?
> **Kk:** so late wor!!!!? i'm working ar!!
> **Jj:** o ic in a hurry?
> **Kk:** no really!! u ?!
> **Jj:** just to check if there is any e-mail to me
> **Kk:** oic why so late online?! study late?! when 's ur lesson tom ar?! how's ur life (mum & sister not here wor) ?!
> **Jj:** 11:30, but have hw to work tom morning
> **Kk:** oic till when ar?!
> **Jj:** 4:30
> **Kk:** oh. . . . so long . . . time?!
> **Jj:** 2 hrs is vacant
> **Kk:** oic u remember to take mobile with battery wor!!! maybe i'll call u gar!!!
> **Jj:** Yes ar, to bring my mobile phone ma
> **Kk:** fine
> **Jj:** i offline la ,bb :-)

Two students chatting online

This extract shows both the advantages and the limitations of online chatting. It is clearly done with enthusiasm and immediacy – two of the characteristics we have identified for a successful building of a writing habit – but it also uses a 'chat' register (with all its attendant abbreviations and informalities) as well as mixing English with Cantonese and written abbreviations to create, in Ken Hyland's words, 'a new hybrid form of discourse'. Students need, as we have said, to be aware of when and where this kind of written communication is appropriate and when it is not.

 Letters backwards and forwards – we can move on from the kinds of notes and e-mails we have been looking at by getting students to write letters to each other – and reply to letters too. We have already mentioned the popular 'agony column' activity (see page 40), but other letters are possible too. Students could read an article and then write a letter to an imaginary newspaper giving their opinion. The letters are then given to different classmates who each have to write to the same imaginary newspaper either agreeing or disagreeing with the letters in front of them. When the letters have been completed, the teacher can display them on the class noticeboard or, better still, the teacher and the students together, using a computer (and if possible, a page-making program), can create their own mocked-up letters page.

Such invented-purpose tasks can be extremely motivating since they give students a reason, however unreal this may appear to be, to write to each other. Just as role-playing can have immense benefits for some students in the development of their oral competence (and give them good rehearsal practice for real-life communication), so too this kind of written role-play can have the same effect.

Any kind of letter where a reply might be expected can be used in this way. A letter of enquiry can be answered by a student who has some information (perhaps provided by the coursebook or the teacher) to send back. A letter of complaint can be answered by someone trying to be emollient (if they want).

Getting students to communicate with each other in writing is one way of building the writing habit in a motivating and realistic way.

What to do with 'habit-building' writing

Although we will deal with responses to student writing in detail in Chapter 7, we should make some comments here about what teachers can do with the results of 'habit-building' writing.

We have stressed that one of the purposes for the writing activities we have been looking at in this chapter is to give students engaging writing tasks that will help them become fluent writers. We have mentioned the benefit that successful production has for students' confidence as writers. And we have seen how students enjoy their own and each other's efforts in examples like the fairy story on page 79 and the poetry activities on pages 69–73.

One answer, therefore, to what we should do with the results of this kind of writing is to let students enjoy them. Let them read and see each other's work; encourage them to read out what they have done or let them put it up on a class website, for example.

Yet, as we have seen, the kind of writing fluency we have been encouraging may well bring mistakes with it. We may not be keen for our students to show work that has such mistakes (for their sake). And because quickly produced work like this presents ideal opportunities for students to have a go with the language at their disposal, it would be silly not to engage in some form of feedback which focused on more formal aspects of grammar and written style.

What teachers need to be able to do, therefore, is help students enjoy their work and take pride in it and, at the same time, use what they have produced for correction without destroying the positive atmosphere which the tasks, hopefully, have created. It is this balance between appropriate acknowledgement and language improvement which we will consider in detail in Chapter 7.

Conclusions   In this chapter we have:
- discussed the desirability of building the writing habit, especially for those who are unused to writing and fear they cannot do it.
- shown how by choosing the right tasks (bearing in mind the need for engagement) students will be keen to write.
- talked about the need to help students to have 'something to say' by giving appropriate task information, necessary language, and, on occasions, patterns and schemes to follow.
- discussed the need to make writing worthwhile – through sharing and displaying written work in some way.
- detailed a number of activities for instant writing including sentence writing, using music, pictures, and poems.
- looked at examples of collaborative writing, stressing the beneficial effects of students working together to produce written text, with or without a scribe.
- looked at ways in which we can get students to write to each other whether by passing notes, by e-mail, in live chat, or by writing simulated letters.
- said that teachers need to give positive acknowledgement as well as more formal language feedback.

Looking ahead
- In the next chapter we will look at writing tasks which involve studying genre and which concentrate more fundamentally on the writing process itself.
- In Chapter 7 we will look in detail at the options available to teachers who want to respond to students' work in a number of different ways.
- The final chapter will look at other uses for writing, including journal keeping.

6 'Worked-on' writing

What is written without effort is read without pleasure.
Samuel Johnson

- ● **Process and genre**
- ● **Generating ideas**
- ● **Analysing genres**
- ● **Making a plan**
- ● **Examples of 'worked-on' writing sequences**
- ● **Project work**
- ● **Writing for exams**

Process and genre

Given that writing is a process and that what we write is often heavily influenced by the constraints of genres, then these elements have to be present in learning activities. Building the writing habit (with activities such as those we looked at in the previous chapter) is extremely important, but without looking at examples of different genres to see how they are constructed, and without becoming used to drafting and re-drafting, students are unlikely to become effective writers.

In past discussions of process and genre, writers tended to think that these two ways of looking at writing were mutually exclusive – that is, teachers either got students to look at written genres or had them concentrate on the writing process itself. Yet there is no good reason why this should be the case. We may feel, for example, that analysing a certain written genre in order to be able to write within that genre is an integral part of the planning stage in a process approach – even if that analysis encourages students and other writers to 'disobey' some of the genre conventions. In the same way we may well get students to concentrate on the writing process – drafting and re-drafting for example – when they are writing within a genre.

The activities in this chapter, therefore, are most often a blend of genre study and process sequences. Sometimes they are more heavily weighted towards the one, sometimes to the other. But what they have in common is that students are asked to think carefully about what they are writing, and then think about and evaluate what they have written. If, over a period of time, these activities are incorporated in a programme that also includes sentence and paragraph writing (see Chapter 4) and 'habit-building' writing (Chapter 5), there is a good chance that students will emerge as competent writers. They will be able to operate in a variety of genres and to address a number of different audiences, producing written work of a high standard.

Furthermore, these activities frequently stimulate genuinely purposeful spoken communication.

Three key first stages in 'process + genre' writing lessons are the generation of ideas, the study of individual genres, and the planning of texts.

Generating ideas

Often, even the most fluent writers in their own language need time to generate ideas and to plan what they are going to write. Students are no different. If we are going to ask them to write anything more substantial than instant writing (see page 63), we have to give them opportunities to think. This is especially true of more formal writing tasks such as narrative writing, discursive writing (offering opposing views on a topic before stating a considered opinion), report writing, formal letter writing, or the design of publicity material such as advertisements and posters.

The following examples show ways of generating ideas (these mostly use collaboration, to make generating ideas more enjoyable and productive) and of noting down ideas:

 The buzz group – by far the most common collaborative model is the buzz group. This is where students 'buzz' or generate ideas, reactions, cues, or opinions quickly and informally. We might ask students to get into groups and quickly come up with five reasons why people prefer cars to public transport. We might ask students to make quick notes about what to put in a composition describing a picture. If they are going to design an advertisement, students can talk and make notes about what they are going to advertise, what main points they want to get over, etc. They could talk about what information needs to go into a biography, or what a good first line (for a novel) should contain.

Buzz groups can be created instantly and they frequently lead to successful idea generation which the individual student can then carry forward into their own planning.

 Individuals, pairs, and groups – a more elaborate version of the buzz group is called 'pyramid planning' by Tricia Hedge. Here students think about a topic individually and then discuss it in pairs and then in groups. Imagine that students are going to write a composition about how to cope with phobias (or about the bravest person they have ever met). They first read a powerful description of someone coping with a phobia (or about someone who is/was really brave). The teacher then sees if anyone wants to tell the class about how they or someone they know deals with phobias (or about someone really brave). Students are then asked to work individually to think about what they might include in a composition on this topic. The teacher might go round helping them with suggestions about, for example, what phobias are, why they happen, and what can be done about them.

Students are now put in pairs to discuss what they think needs to be included in their composition. When they have had time to talk, groups are formed with each member of the group coming from a different pair. The result is that ideas and possibilities are shared among the greatest number of students. By the time the teacher asks the students to report back on their ideas, everyone has had the opportunity not only to make suggestions but also to have their imaginations stimulated by the suggestions of others.

 Whole group discussion – sometimes students need help not only with having ideas and thinking of a topic they might want to write about, but also with thinking of appropriate vocabulary.

In Aosta, Italy, Francesca Acanfora wanted her students to write Haiku and other kinds of poetry. To get them to do this she first allowed them to suggest themes that they wanted to write about, thus ensuring their engagement and co-operation. She then asked students to give her any words they knew which could be used in that topic area. These were transferred to the board according to their grammatical classes (verbs, nouns, adjectives, adverbs, etc.). The students now had the raw material for their poetry:

Say a word And my heart thunders I'm completely confused. (Stefania, 18)	Had I one night without you I'd touch emptyness … I refuse that thought (Alessandra, 20)

From *Haiku ed altre poesie* edited by Francesca Albarosa Acanfora

This kind of whole-group preparation – discussing issues, eliciting and sharing useful words and grammar, getting students engaged in the activity – need not be confined to poetry, of course. The same procedure could be followed when preparing to design advertisements (eliciting topic words and phrases, looking at advertisements and commenting on them, etc.) or stories (how should a story start, what kind of a resolution should it have, etc.).

 Note making – students benefit greatly from thinking about how best to note down the ideas they come up with. Indeed the effective making of notes can contribute to the generation of ideas themselves.

Often, when we start to generate ideas we write down words and phrases in a random way. Then, by making connections between them, we start to see patterns emerging and we can then organise our thoughts into sub-topics and categories. This is a classic note-making sequence.

A mistake some teachers have made in the past is to try to impose, in the most helpful way, a method of making notes. Yet just as each person may have different preferences (for music, or visual stimuli, for example), so the way we make notes is an extremely personal affair. It is much better, therefore, to expose students to a variety of note-making options and then let them choose the one they find most useful – or indeed some other system that suits them.

Some people, for example, prefer a **spaghetti** approach:

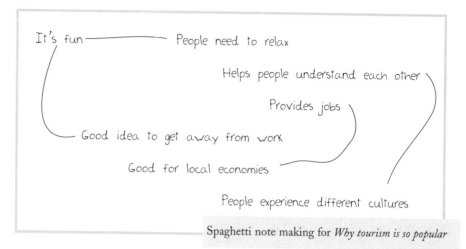

Spaghetti note making for *Why tourism is so popular*

Another very visual way of making preparation notes is often referred to as a **spidergram** or **mind map**. In this idea-generating model students start with a topic at the centre and then generate a web of ideas from that.

If the students are generating ideas on the subject of holidays, for example, they might produce a spidergram like this (either individually, or in small or large groups):

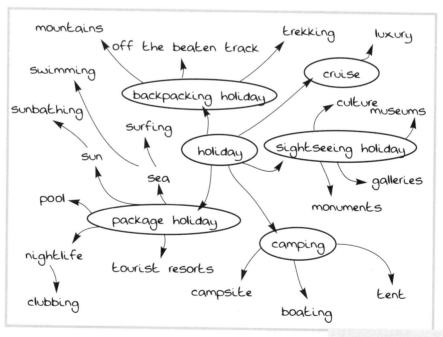

Spidergram for *holidays*

Spidergrams work (for some students) because their visual design allows students to extend their ideas in any direction they want while, at the same time, encouraging them to group themes and sub-themes together as they proceed. Spidergrams work especially well when students create spidergrams in groups since the discussion this engenders together with its visual representation helps to stimulate creativity. But it is also interesting for individual students to show each other their own spidergrams and see how similar they are (or not).

Some students, however, may prefer to make a list of **ordered points**:

Are holidays good for you?

1   Introduction
     a   More and more people go on holiday
     b   Holidays are cheaper than ever
     c   People think they have a right to holidays

2   Why we like holidays
     a   A chance to get away from it all
     b   A chance to get to know other people/cultures
     c   Physical exercise/fresh air

3   Holiday problems
     a   People often sunbathe, eat, & drink too much
     b   Travelling can be stressful

Ordered points for *Are holidays good for you?*

For and against – another way of generating ideas, especially where the writing is to be discursive or will consider different arguments, is to generate **for and against** notes. Suppose, for example, that our students were going to write a composition entitled 'Is tourism good for us?', we might separate the class into two buzz groups. The first group has five minutes to think of as many ideas as they can about why tourism is a good thing; the second group has to think of as many ideas as they can about why tourism is a bad thing. The teacher can then divide the board into two columns, a 'for' and an 'against' column, and representatives from each group come up and write their points on the correct side of the board.

The students (and board) do not have to be divided in this way, of course. They can work individually or in pairs to generate their own 'for' and 'against' lists of points – which they can then share with the class. We might start by giving the same kind of table about tourism as we did for mobile phones (see page 53), only this time they have to generate four more ideas for each side of the table once we have started them off with some possibilities.

We could, alternatively, start the for-and-against board filling with the whole class; any student can come up to the board and write something in the 'for' or 'against' column as soon as an idea occurs to them. We can set up flip charts around the room and have students write up points under different headings, and so on.

The important thing with all these kinds of activities is that they make students think, and provide them with the ideas and words they will need to complete their written tasks.

Analysing genres

Where students are writing within a recognised genre, they will benefit from first analysing that genre before writing within it – although we do not want them to be straitjacketed by it, of course.

If students are looking at newspapers, for example, we will want them to analyse an article or a review to find out what the writer is trying to achieve. What functions are the different paragraphs performing? (The first paragraph in a current affairs news article, for example, generally sums up the whole of what is to follow.) What noticeable language features can the students identify? Is there anything special about the vocabulary being used, or about the punctuation, or the layout? If students are looking at advertisements, they can analyse some examples of written advertisements, using a list of questions like these:

ANALYSING ADVERTISEMENTS

Answer the following questions about the advertisement you are reading:

MEANING
What is being advertised?
Who do you think the advertisement is aimed at?
What's the main message about the product or service?
What captions are included in the advertisement? How effective are they?
What visual material does the advertisement use? How effective is it?
Is this a good advertisement? Why?

(LANGUAGE) CONSTRUCTION
What vocabulary describes the product or service?
What form do the captions take?
What verb tenses are used? Why?
What words or phrases are new to you?
What is the structure of the advertisement (e.g. caption, description, story, background, etc.)?

Genre analyser for *advertisements*

A crucial question within the genre analyser is who the advertisement is for; this concern with **audience** is vital when looking at examples of writing. It means we understand why a writer used formal or informal language, or why some words were chosen rather than others (see page 25). When we know who a text is written for, the way in which the information is presented (and the language which is used) makes more sense. Understanding the relationship between the intended audience and the layout and language choice of the writer will help students when they come to write their own pieces.

Teachers can ask students to analyse example texts either before, during, or after an idea-generation phase. The important thing is for them to gain insights into how text is constructed and how language is typically used.

Making a plan

Generating ideas and analysing genres are all part of the planning process but they are, of course, different from the act of making a plan itself. It is here that students decide what order to put their ideas in, and how best to present their information.

One of the first decisions that students have to make is who they are writing for – however real or invented their purpose is. This will help them with the overall design of the text they are preparing. Then they can move on to considering how to organise their ideas. Although this is a personal business, nevertheless we can help them think about how ideas group round themes in the following ways:

 For and against – we have seen how students can group opinions in 'for' and 'against' columns when they are planning a discursive essay. Once they have done this, we can ask them how they wish to order the 'for' points and how to order the 'against' points. Do they think the most powerful argument should come first? Which is the most powerful argument in their opinion?

Having decided the order of arguments on either side they then need to decide which order 'for' and 'against' will be presented in, and how the composition can start, and how it will end.

 Board fill – when students have worked together to generate ideas, we can ask them to write them on the board (or to dictate them so that we write the ideas for them). The ideas are written up in no particular order, until the board is covered with words, phrases, and sentences. Students then agree with the teacher about which ideas go together by drawing lines to connect them. We end up with something like a spidergram but, because we started with ideas which had already been generated, we can focus all our attention on how they group together.

 Main idea magnets – when students have had a chance to think of ideas, they can decide on four main points which are then written up on the board. They then have to come up to the board and write all the other ideas next to the 'main idea magnets' – unless they don't fit, in which case they can be put into a special 'extras' category at one side of the board. Once again we are drawing attention to how ideas group together.

At the end of the activity students can decide what to do with any ideas that end up in the 'extras' column. Perhaps they need a fifth or sixth 'magnet'. Perhaps some of the ideas can be jettisoned without having too great an impact on the whole.

 Papers in a hat – students can be given a topic and asked, individually, to think of one idea and write it on a piece of paper. All the pieces of paper are then put into a box and mixed up. The pieces of paper are then removed, and the students have to work out how they are connected and how they might be made into a composition.

Apart from 'Papers in a hat', all the above activities are teacher- and board-focused. There is a good reason for this: it allows all the students to get a clear understanding of this aspect of making a plan. However, such activities can also be done by students working in pairs or groups, using paper and (marker) pens.

As with all plans, however, things can change during the drafting and editing process. Points may be reordered, or they may attach themselves to different headings. Having seen what the results of a plan look like, the student might well start the piece of writing completely differently. The end might look better at the beginning! The 'for' and 'against' arguments might be reversed. That is all part of the writing process.

Examples of 'worked-on' writing sequences

The following examples show a range of 'genre + process' activities. In some of them students think carefully about what they are going to write before they start. In others they study the genre that they are going to write in, and in others opportunities are provided for rewriting, re-planning, re-editing, etc. Some of the activities here include all of these elements. Others concentrate on specific aspects of the writing process.

One element of the writing process that does not receive much attention here is editing (or self-evaluating), a crucial factor of the process cycle (see the **process wheel** on page 6). This will be discussed in detail in the next chapter.

Example 1: Writing within a genre – 'guidebooks' (elementary, pre-intermediate)

Imitation guidebooks are extremely useful for worked-on writing particularly because they encompass a range of functions: description, information, advice, and recommendation. They can be worked on at various levels, including at elementary and pre-intermediate levels, as in this example.

The activity begins when the teacher holds up a number of guidebooks and establishes that the students know what they are. The teacher then elicits from the class what a guidebook contains, and ends up with a list which might look something like this:

> *Places* – buildings, parks, rivers, bridges, museums, etc.
> *History* – history of a place, history of buildings
> *Food* – typical food
> *Culture* – music, dances, festivals
> *Things to buy* – leather, silver, pottery, etc.
> *Entertainment* – restaurants, night clubs, theatre, music, etc.
> *Climate* – hot, cold, windy, etc.

The class then decides where they are going to write a guidebook for. It might be the place where the class is taking place; if students have access to the Internet, on the other hand, they can decide on other places they want to write a guidebook for.

In groups, students now decide on one or two facts for each of the categories mentioned above. All they have to do is write a sentence or two about it, using as much language as they can muster, e.g.

> The Hermitage Museum is an important building in St Petersburg.
>
> or
>
> The Miramar Restaurant is a good restaurant for fish in Port D'Alcudia.
>
> etc.

The teacher then shows students models of guidebooks, either in the students' own language, in English, or in simplified form so that the layout is easy to explain. Students understand that guidebook entries often start with a general introduction about a place (e.g. *Fortaleza is on the north-east coast of Brazil in the state of Ceara*). They then go on to discuss different aspects of the place (e.g. places to visit, places to eat, etc.).

Students start to organise their own 'guidebooks', e.g.

> Places to visit:
>
> Buckingham Palace (the Queen lives there)
> The South Bank (concert hall, art galleries, and restaurants)
> Hyde Park
>
> etc.

They then go on to write their own books or sections of books (e.g. 'local food' only) about the place they have chosen.

There are a number of points that we need to consider about this sequence. In the first place, it includes planning, genre analysis, etc. Secondly, the sequence can last for varying amounts of time; it can, for example, be extended into a full-blown project (see pages 103–104) which can last over two or three lessons (or even weeks). Thirdly, tasks can be shared between groups so that one group, for example, can write about places to visit while another group can write about entertainment. Finally, what the students produce will depend upon their level but, as we have shown, it is perfectly possible for students at even very low levels to produce meaningful 'worked-on' writing.

In writing tasks such as this, the teacher's support is vitally important. Students will need help with vocabulary, they will need advice about layout, and they will need encouragement to keep going.

Example 2: Writing for different audiences (intermediate and above)

One of the aspects of writing appropriately within a genre is to know who it is you are writing for. For example, students might be asked to study the following newspaper photograph and article about a snowstorm that created chaos one night in Britain:

Big freeze brings travel chaos

Drivers trapped in gridlock overnight as temperatures drop below 2°C

Drivers in parts of the country hit by snow and ice were today warned only to drive if absolutely necessary after the big freeze caused gridlocks and travel chaos.

Some commuters reported still being stuck in a horrendous traffic jam on the M11 in Essex and Cambridgeshire this morning, having set off to travel home from work yesterday evening.

Forecasters said that snow was still falling in Norfolk, Suffolk and parts of north Yorkshire this morning. London and the southeast are set to clear but, with temperatures expected to remain below 2°C (35.6°F), roads are likely to remain dangerously icy, PA Weather Centre warned.

The M11 remained closed this morning between junction eight northbound and junction nine southbound, Essex police said. The motorway was blocked last night by a series of accidents, jack-knifed lorries and abandoned cars, and police are advising motorists not to use the M11 or A14 as both remain "impassable".

A spokesman for Cambridge police said that the M11 is "effectively a car park", adding: "Roads are completely congested and extremely dangerous this morning."

From *Guardian Unlimited* at www.guardian.co.uk

Students now discuss the news item and in particular think about the plight of people who were trapped in their cars all night. The teacher then asks them to look at the following written tasks:

> a   Write an e-mail from a truck driver who has only just got home after being stranded for 24 hours. He is e-mailing his friend.
>
> b   Write an e-mail from the same driver to his employer explaining why he has not been able to make a scheduled delivery.
>
> c   Write a text message from a driver to his girlfriend/wife when he became stuck in the storm.
>
> d   Write a report by the transport authority about the extent of the problem and what needs to be done to prevent it happening in the future.

Ideally, before this session, the students have looked at examples of text messages and discussed how they are 'written'. They can then write appropriately in that genre for task **c**. They have looked at e-mail writing before too, noting its various characteristics. As a result, in task **a** they will probably include short verbless phrases, use exclamation marks, and perhaps even emoticons. They will know that his e-mail to his employer, on the other hand, will be significantly more formal in tone. And they will know that the report (in task **d**) will need to follow a conventional report structure.

This activity emphasises the genre aspect of writing. It can form the basis for more than one lesson. Different students can write different versions of the story in the different genres, and they can build up a whole 'blizzard' project focusing on the different ways it can be written about.

Example 3: Research and writing – 'biography' (intermediate and above)

This activity sequence shows how a mix of genre and process work can enable students to write short biographies of people who interest them. It shows, too, how writing can fit into a wider learning sequence. At one stage it uses Internet access, but the sequence can work just as well with more traditional reference tools, such as encyclopaedias.

Before this reading–writing sequence starts, students are (re-)exposed to the vocabulary of history and biography (e.g. *guilty, prison, sentence* (verb), *disguise, escape, pirate, soldier, capture, die, execute, inherit*).

Students then each read one of three biography texts about someone famous (or infamous!). They fill in this table about the person they have read about and then, by asking people who have read about the other two people, they complete the other columns about those two as well:

	1	2	3
Name			
Date of birth			
Nationality			
What was or is special about her/him?			
Who (if anyone) was or is she/he associated with?			
What were or have been the main events in her/his life?			
Has her/his career ended, and if yes, how?			
Are they still alive, and if not, when did she/he die?			

Biography table

Once the teacher has led feedback on the task – getting students to talk about the information in their tables, and checking they have understood the texts they have read and what their fellow students have told them – they are asked to make a new (empty) version of the table. They then take their table with them to a computer room where they log onto a biography site on the Internet, such as the one at www.biography.com. Once there, they can type in the name of anyone they want to find out about, either living or dead. When they find the person they are looking for, they fill in their table about them. They should be told not to try and write down the whole text but, by using the table, to make notes only.

While they are doing this, the teacher can go from computer to computer helping students with vocabulary they do not understand.

Once the students have finished taking notes, they leave the computer screens and go back to the classroom where they use their notes to write short biographies. When they have completed their first draft, they can show what they have done to their teacher. In one use of this activity, one student wrote (about the singer Ricky Martin), *His career haven't finished. I think his career is starting now. He's very young, he's still alive.* The teacher asked her to check the verb in the first sentence, and to think about the second sentence (because his career had already started). Another student (still fascinated by Princess Diana) wrote, *She attended the clusive West Heath boarding school,* and the teacher was able to ask that student to go back to the computer room to see if that's what she had found there. Still another student wrote the following, about the British Prime Minister Tony Blair, *Between 1967–1983 he specialized in employment and industrial law and joined the labour party in 1976, main course – nationalisation of industry and increased powder of trade union –*

James Callaghan. She could not remember, from her notes, exactly what she meant and so she, too, went back to the computer room to check.

It should not be assumed that all the teacher's comments were negative. On the contrary, there was much to be impressed by and many other suggestions to be made. But these few examples show how, in the right circumstances, teacher advice can point students in the direction of successful re-drafting.

The final versions of the biographies were much better. About Ricky Martin the student now wrote, *His career has not yet finished. It has only just started. He's very young, he's still very much alive.* Princess Diana now had attended an *exclusive school,* and Tony Blair *had been worried, when he joined the Labour Party in 1976, about nationalisation and the power of the trade union movement.*

The final biographies that the students produce may not be perfect, but in one or two class periods they have investigated a particular genre ('short encyclopaedic biographies') and have been able to put what they have learnt into practice. As well as this they have been able to work on their own writing, drafting and re-drafting, so that their final versions, which they show to their classmates and which are discussed by the whole group, should be of a high standard for their level.

Of course, biography.com is not the only website for such an activity. There are various other encyclopaedia-type places to go to, such as www.britannica.com. Higher-level students can make use of a search engine such as Google (www.google.com); by typing in the name of the person they want to research, they will get a long list of sites where they can find relevant information.

Or can they? A potential risk with search engines is that if the searcher is not careful, he or she will be inundated with 'hits', some or many of which may not be directly relevant to the research topic. This can be a problem for everybody, of course, not just students of English. For example, if the student who is interested in Ricky Martin just types the singer's name into a search engine, she is likely to get a list of well over a million separate items, including record store sites, fan pages, official sites, gossip magazines, MTV listings, and so on. As a result, she will find it almost impossible to choose between sites with such variable relevance to her specific research topic. However, if she were to type 'life facts Ricky Martin' (words like *and* and *of* are not worth putting in) and to hit 'return', a search engine would offer her a much smaller list of sites and pages. Almost all of them would now offer potted biographies or articles about the singer's life. Searching is an art, in other words, and before we get students to do this kind of task we need to make sure that they will search skilfully so that they get maximum benefit from the activity.

Example 4: Extended writing – 'personal narrative' (upper intermediate and above)

Many of the ideas we have discussed so far come together in the following writing procedure described by Linda Pearce from the University of the Western Cape in South Africa. When students first arrive at the university, she and her colleagues need to get them accustomed to writing essays. The genre they start with is the 'narrative essay' which is a useful stage towards the writing of discursive essays, although for the students she describes it was, for some time, quite sensitive given the history of apartheid which they had all lived through. However, staff at the university thought that story telling, especially about difficult events in the students' past, had a cathartic effect.

What follows is a description of how attention to genre norms and constraints is mixed seamlessly with aspects of the **process wheel** discussed in Chapter 1. The whole procedure (which takes place over two sessions) has seven distinct stages:

- **Stage 1** – in pairs or groups, students talk about any vivid memories from their childhood. While they are doing this, the teacher writes sentences on the board such as:

> I remember when the dog had ten puppies under my bed.
> I remember the night of the great storm when the house was flooded.
> I remember when the police raided the school and my brother was arrested.

Students are then asked to look at the board examples and then write their own similar *I remember* sentences.

- **Stage 2** – students talk about two types of **freewriting** (something they have had a go at before). 'Free' freewriting is just that. Students have to start writing about anything for a fixed period of time (if they can't think of anything to write, they just keep writing *I can't think of anything to write* until they do!). 'Guided' freewriting is the same thing, only this time students think of a topic before they start. In this case, for example, students can take the *I remember* sentences they have written and extend them as much and as far as they can.

- **Stage 3** – the teacher puts a **cluster** diagram, very like a spidergram, on the board which suggests certain aspects of childhood memory (see 1 on page 100).

   The students now read finished 'childhood memories' essays written by students in previous years. Taking one particular one of these, they and the teacher use this diagram to identify different parts of the story (see 2 on page 100).

- **Stage 4** – the students now make their own diagrams about their own childhood memories. They then use their previous freewriting and their cluster diagrams to write the first draft of their essay.

- **Stage 5** – the students now read three more finished essays written by former students – ones that the teachers consider to be good examples of the genre.

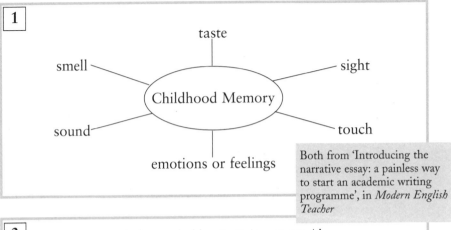

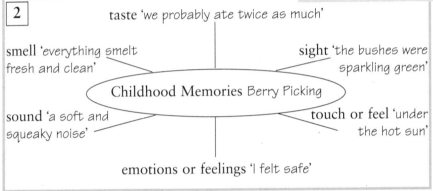

Both from 'Introducing the narrative essay: a painless way to start an academic writing programme', in *Modern English Teacher*

- **Stage 6** – the students work through a handout which asks them to look back at their first draft and asks them questions such as these:

> **Is the beginning interesting?**
> **Does it make you want to read on?**
> **Does it prepare you for what is going to come next?**

There are other questions and suggestions, too, all designed to get students looking at their first drafts carefully to see how they might be improved. They also look at the beginnings of two of the former students' stories to see how they wrote their narratives.

- **Stage 7** – the class then discuss everything they have been doing and that they have seen, clearing up any questions about narrative construction and style. Now they are ready to go away and write the next – and perhaps final – draft of the narrative.

**Example 5: Writing within a genre – 'advertising leaflets'
(upper intermediate and above)**

When students design advertisements, posters, and leaflets, they need to be well-informed about the best ways of doing this. In the following leaflet activity, therefore, students look at an example of a typical leaflet such as the one shown on the next page.

To start with, students study the leaflet shown on page 102 and say what 'Aroma' is and what it does. They discuss whether any of the courses on offer interest them a lot, a little, not much, or not at all. They are then asked to look at the design of the leaflet and complete the following tasks:

a   Do you think it is effective?
b   What is the purpose of the front cover? Would you design a cover like that?
c   Do you like the use of 'bullet' points? Are they easy to read and notice?
d   How important are the photographs on the back?

On the basis of this leaflet – and any others which the students or the teacher bring into the class – students can discuss what a good leaflet should contain, and what they think it needs to look like in order to attract people's attention.

They are then told to choose between a number of alternatives (e.g. a centre for music tuition, a new gym, a new school cafeteria, etc.) and to start to think about content and design by completing a table like this one:

Questions/topics to be decided	Notes/decisions
What kind of a place is it?	
The name of the place (think up something interesting)	
What services the place offers (and brief explanations of what these services are)	
Names of the staff	
An address, phone number, website address, etc.	

Preparation table

They then write the text for the leaflet based on their notes in the table. They discuss what they have written and maybe show it to other students for their suggestions and/or corrections. Finally they fold a piece of A4 paper in half (or in three), and decide what text goes where, and what pictures and designs to include. Once again they continually edit and modify the text and the design until they are happy with the result.

AROMA'S STAFF

Sally Grace, NAL,
Director

Justin Norris, FSDE

Helena Kollect, CCE

Contact Aroma at:
The Aroma Centre,
26 Carper Row,
Middleton Cleethorpe,
Lancs LT6 5YW
Tel: 01672 462057
Email:enquiries@arofengcol.com
Web site: www.arofengcol.com

Courses in:

Aromatherapy • How different smells affect our mood
• Designing aroma zones
• Judging the best aromas on the market

Feng Shui* • The theory of Feng Shui explained
• Putting Feng Shui to work at home
• Putting Feng Shui to work at work

Relaxing colour • How colour affects our mood
• Colour combinations
• Designing rooms with colour in mind

*Feng Shui is the ancient Chinese science which tells
people the best place to put furniture in a room or house for
maximum comfort, good luck and success.

Based on an activity from *Just Right: Upper Intermediate* by Jeremy Harmer and Carol Lethaby

Project work We use the word *project* to describe pieces of work which extend over a period of time, and where the final product may be the result of considerable research.

Project work has long been popular in English language teaching and learning, although its use is naturally constrained by the amount of time available for its implementation. One of the most widely discussed examples of project work took place in the city of Bath, UK. There, students at the Bell School compiled, over a period of time, a 'wheelchair user's guide' to the city based on visits to public buildings and spaces, on interviews, and on research about the needs of wheelchair-bound citizens. The guide that was produced was a genuinely useful document, and it is this fact that made the students' work particularly valuable for the students themselves and for people in Bath.

There are many possible areas for project work, such as producing a class newspaper, guides to a town, or 'books' on historical or cultural topics. Some projects look at people's attitudes to current issues, while in others students are asked to produce brochures for a public service or a new company.

What these examples demonstrate is that the difference between a full-blown project and the kind of examples that we have been looking at in this chapter so far is chiefly one of time and scale. The production of the leaflet (pages 101–102) was a kind of mini-project, as were the biography sequence (pages 96–98) and the 'childhood memories' essays (pages 98–100). The finished result of a full-blown project is more substantial than an essay or a story of a few hundred words. But being more extensive, they need careful planning and implementation.

Project procedures

However projects are organised, they all share the same basic sequence:

- **The choice/the briefing** – students may choose what they want to do a project on, or the teacher may offer one or more project topics. Once the choice has been made, a briefing takes place in which teacher and students define the aims of the project and discuss how they can gather data, what the timescale of the project is, what stages it will go through, and what support the students will get as the work progresses.

- **Idea/language generation** – once a briefing has taken place, students start on the process of idea generation. What is going to go into their projects? What do they need to find out? What words or language are particularly useful for the topic area they are working in?

- **Data gathering** – students can gather data from a number of sources. They can consult encyclopaedias or go to the Internet to find what they are looking for. They can design questionnaires so that they can interview people. They can look at texts for genre analysis or watch television programmes, especially documentaries, and take notes about the information that is given there.

- **Planning** – when students have got their ideas, generated some topic-specific language, and gathered the data they require, they can start to make a plan of how the final project will be set out.

- **Drafting and editing** – the project is now drafted out, with either sections or the whole thing produced so that they can be looked at by fellow students or by the teacher – as well as being self-edited by the project writers.

- **Final version** – when the final version has been produced, the different class projects can be gathered together and displayed in the school library or in some part of the classroom. They can be shown to other classes. The important thing is for them to be displayed and read by as many people as possible. There must be some payoff for so much work.

- **Consultation/tutorial** – throughout the lifetime of a project teachers will need to be available as tutors, advising, helping, and 'prodding' students to help them progress. Such consultations will, of course, focus on drafts and how to edit them successfully, but they may also help students to come up with ideas when they get stuck. A frequent problem occurs when students try to do too much in a project, so teachers may need to help them narrow down the focus of their work.

Although not always feasible (principally, perhaps, because of limitations of time), projects are an excellent way to combine genre study with work on the writing process. They involve detailed planning and idea generation. They encourage students to gather data and they provoke significant planning, drafting, and editing too. And at the end of everything, students have work they can show proudly to others.

Writing for exams

Most public exams for students of English include a written element. A student's writing will often allow the examiner to get a better picture of their overall language ability than a test of specific language points does, for example.

One of the teacher's most important roles will be to prepare students for the writing they will have to do in exams. In order to do this, however, we need to be absolutely clear about what those tasks are likely to be, and what will be expected of the examinee.

Types of exam writing

Among the many different kinds of exam tasks that are currently in use, the following are some of the most common:

- Application letters and CVs
- Articles, reports, and reviews
- Descriptions of pictures, paintings, or events
- Discursive compositions
- Leaflets
- Letters (informal and formal)
- Narratives (often the first or last line is given)

- Transactional letters (where candidates have to respond to specific information in the question, or give specific details as requested)

Preparing students for exam writing

However good an exam is at testing general language ability, the tasks that students are asked to do may still come as a surprise if those students have not been prepared for the exam. Most tests have their own special features, and if we want our students to do as well as they are capable of, they need to have a familiarity with those specialities. They also need to be prompted to use their best planning and editing skills in an exam situation. Among the things we need to offer students, therefore, are the following:

- **Model answers** – students need to see what is expected of them. One way of doing this is to show them model answers – ones that would satisfy the examiners of the papers they are aiming to sit. These model answers should not be thought of as straitjackets, but rather as frameworks which students can lean on to help them. As with all the examples in this chapter which asked students to analyse a genre, the teacher will want to draw out aspects of the model – such as what kind of information is included in the first paragraph, or what kind of language is used to introduce a topic, sign off from a letter, or add contrasting opinions.

- **Reading instructions** – a crucial issue for all exam candidates is to understand what they are being asked to do. This sounds obvious and yet many candidates fail because they do not read instruction rubrics carefully enough. Sometimes, as we have seen, they are asked to include information in their answers or to mention certain specific topics. They will obviously be penalised if they fail to do these things.

  Teachers need to stress the importance of reading instructions carefully and should, therefore, give students considerable practice in reading and interpreting instruction rubrics both on their own (the teacher can get them to say exactly what it is they are being asked to do) and as part of exam-practice writing.

- **Generating ideas and plans** – although it is easier to generate ideas and plans when working in pairs or groups, students need to be encouraged to do their own 'internal' brainstorming, note making, and planning. Just because they are on their own in an exam room, this does not mean that they cannot use the skills they have acquired in idea generation and in planning.

  One way of helping students to get used to the planning phase in exams is to give them, repeatedly, tasks which they have to plan for individually. This can be done in any free five minutes, say at the beginning or end of the lesson. Students can be asked to compare their different ideas and see who has come up with what sounds the best plan. All the idea-generating ideas at the beginning of this chapter can be used with exam tasks.

- **Writing** – when students write in exams they need to be able to do so quickly but not carelessly. One way of encouraging this ability is to set timed essays and compositions at various stages of the teaching cycle. This will give students a feel for the kind of writing they will need to do in exams.

If there is not enough space in the timetable for this kind of activity, students can be asked to do timed essays for homework. The teacher should explain clearly why this is important, and give exact times. It is then up to the students to take advantage of these practice opportunities when and if they want to.

- **Revising** – students who do not read through what they have written in an exam situation (in order to make changes and correct mistakes) are at a great disadvantage. However good their writing has been, they will almost certainly have made some errors.

  Teachers need to give students practice in checking through their work. We will be looking at examples of this in the next chapter and show how we can train students to edit their drafted work. In exam terms we can give them examples of other students' work for them to correct. We can have students swap each other's exam tasks so that they then check someone else's work. We can collect first drafts and give them back to the students one or two classes later, so that they can read through their work with the advantage that the distance of time offers them. All of these things will help build the habit of editing.

- **Mock exams and practice papers** – where possible, students should always have a chance to take mock exams, where they have to complete realistic exam tasks in a realistic exam setting. We do not want them to go into the actual exam and be shocked by the unfamiliarity of it. In the same way students can work through practice papers and questions. Sometimes, as with timed work, this can be done in class, sometimes at home.

Conclusions

In this chapter we have:
- reminded ourselves of the importance of written genre and the writing process in the teaching of writing.
- said that, ideally, in activities where we intend to focus on the writing skill (rather than building writing habits, for example), we should combine attention to genre with a process approach to writing.
- looked at a number of ways that students can be encouraged to generate ideas for their writing.
- shown how genre analysis can help students during the planning process.
- described how the students' attention can be drawn to the making of a specific plan.
- offered five examples of writing sequences where students are encouraged to be creative, are asked to pay attention to genre, and where the writing process includes editing and evaluation.
- discussed project work – an extended version of genre- and process-centred writing.

- talked briefly about writing for exams, detailing some examination tasks and showing what teachers can do to help their students prepare for test activities.

Looking ahead

- In the next chapter we will look at how students can be encouraged to edit their own and others' work. We will discuss the correction of written work and how it can be effected in a constructive and sympathetic way.
- In the final chapter we will look at how writing can be used to help students to reflect and learn.

7 Responding, correcting, and guiding

A man who has committed a mistake and doesn't correct it is committing another mistake.
Confucius

- Ways of reacting to students' writing

- Ways of correcting students' work

- Ways of responding to students' work

- Peer review

- Training students to self-edit and self-correct

- Making homework successful

Ways of reacting to students' writing

In previous chapters it has been suggested that, at various stages in a writing activity, teachers should intervene with editorial comment, motivating suggestions, or language advice. Students, indeed, expect feedback on what they are doing or what they have done.

The ways we react to students' work will depend not only on the kind of task the students are given, but also on what we want to achieve at any one point. There are a number of ways of reacting (as we shall see) but these generally fall within one of two broad categories: responding or correcting.

Responding and correcting

When **responding** to our students' work we are not only concerned with the accuracy of their performance but also – and this is crucial – with the content and design of their writing. We might respond, for example, to the order in which they have made their points ('Why did you start with the story about the bus that was late? You could have begun, instead, with the problem of public transport in general.'). We might respond by saying how much we enjoyed reading their work – and then recommend that the student have a look at a book or website which has more information about the same topic. When responding, we are entering into a kind of affective dialogue with the students. That is, we are discussing their writing rather than judging it.

Correcting, on the other hand, is the stage at which we indicate when something is not right. We correct mistakes in the students' written performance on issues such as **syntax** (word order), **concord** (grammatical agreement between subjects and verbs), **collocation** (words which live together), or word choice.

In a 'process-writing' sequence, where the teacher's intervention is designed to help students edit and move forward to a new draft, responding is often more appropriate than correcting. Our task is not to say what is unequivocally right or wrong, but to ask questions, make suggestions, and indicate where improvements might be made to both the content of the writing and the manner in which it is expressed. Feedback of this kind becomes more and more appropriate as the students' level improves and they can take advantage of such help. However, when students hand in a piece of homework we may mark it to show how correct the writing has been. This will often be the case with 'writing-for-learning' activities (see Chapter 3) and 'nuts and bolts' tasks (see Chapter 4).

The roles of the teacher

When teachers give feedback on students' written performance, they are called on to play a number of different roles. Chris Tribble suggests that at one extreme they will be seen by students as the **examiner**. Almost all teachers will set class tests or mark practice papers for the public exams their students are taking. The students will justifiably expect some kind of an objective evaluation of their performance. This role contrasts strongly with the teacher's potential as the **audience**, responding to the ideas and perceptions that the students have written about. Between these two extremes the teacher may act as an **assistant** (helping the student along), a **resource** (being available when students need information or guidance), an **evaluator** (saying how well things are going so far), or an **editor** (helping to select and rearrange pieces of writing for some kind of publication – whether in or beyond the classroom).

Students are often inclined to see the teacher as an examiner more than anything else. This is hardly surprising since it is generally teachers who mark tests and make decisions about final grades. It is therefore important to show that this is not the only role we can fulfil, especially when students are engaged in a 'writing-for-writing' activity (see page 34).

Who responds?

The previous discussion has assumed that it is always the teacher who gives feedback by responding or correcting. But this is not the case. We can also encourage students to look at each other's work and give advice and make suggestions about how it could be improved. Students become, in effect, their colleagues' audience and, sometimes, their evaluators. Such **peer review** is, as we shall see, an important element in writing activities.

What students do

Responding to students' work – and correcting it – only becomes useful if the students can do something with this feedback. This may just be the encouragement they receive from an enthusiastic teacher or from their peers – encouragement that spurs them on. But where suggestions have been made, we expect students to at least consider their work in the light of these suggestions – and maybe act on the advice which is given.

When teachers return corrected work to their students, they should ensure that the students do not immediately put it to one side, with only a cursory glance at the grade and some of the mistakes. Good correction methods include ensuring that the students understand what the mistakes are and how they can be corrected – if possible, there and then.

As teachers it is our task to make sure students derive as much benefit as possible from our and others' reactions to their writing. However, we need to bear in mind that not all students – indeed not all writers – are as good at editing as others. Not all students are good at letting their mistakes work for them. In the end it is, to an extent, up to them to decide how much they want to (or can) take from what we or their peers suggest.

Ways of correcting students' work

Perhaps the most common way of correcting students' work has been to return it to students with a great deal of underlining, crossings-out, question marks, and the occasional tick. There may be a place for such correction, especially in test marking for example, but this kind of intensive correction can be counter-productive. There are a number of more effective ways of making correction a positive and useful experience.

Selective correction

A way of avoiding the proliferation of red ink all over a student's work is through selective correction. In other words, we do not have to correct everything. We could correct only verb tenses or only punctuation, or focus instead exclusively on word order. We might only correct paragraph organisation or the use of appropriate levels of formality. We might only correct two of the paragraphs in a composition, or only highlight mistakes in the layout of a letter.

If we are going to employ a selective approach, students need to know about it. When we tell them that this time we are only going to be looking at punctuation, they will then concentrate on that aspect of writing especially, something that otherwise they might not do. Selective correction is a good learning tool, in other words.

A way of making selective correction really effective is to discuss with students what the teacher should be looking out for. If they are part of the decision-making process, they are likely to approach the task with more commitment and enthusiasm than usual, and they will pay a great deal of attention to the area earmarked for the teacher's correction.

Using marking scales

Many teachers use a range of different marking scales when correcting written work and written tests. This means that though students may fall down on, say, grammar, they can still perhaps do well in the way they answer a task or in their use of vocabulary.

Teachers may want to give marks out of 10 for each category they have chosen for students (e.g. grammar, vocabulary, coherence, or cohesion). Together with indications of mistakes (where they occur), such marking scales will help students to focus on the particular areas they need to work at.

Using correction symbols

In order to avoid an overabundance of red ink, many teachers use correction symbols. These also have the advantage of encouraging students to think about what the mistake is, so that they can correct it themselves. Many coursebooks include correction symbols in their writing training too.

There is no set list of symbols. Different teachers and coursebooks have their own ways of expressing different concepts. However, the following symbols are frequently used:

Symbol	Meaning	Example error
S	A spelling error	*The asnwer is obvius.*
WO	A mistake in word order	*I like very much it.*
G	A grammar mistake	*I am going to buy some furnitures.*
T	Wrong verb tense	*I have seen him yesterday.*
C	Concord mistake (e.g. subject and verb agreement)	*People is angry.*
⋏	Something has been left out.	*He told ⋏ that he was sorry.*
WW	Wrong word	*I am interested on jazz music.*
{ }	Something is not necessary.	*He was not {too} strong enough.*
?M	The meaning is unclear.	*That is a very excited photograph.*
P	A punctuation mistake	*Do you like London.*
F/I	Too formal or informal	*Hi Mr Franklin, Thank you for your letter ...*

Correction symbols

The teacher writes the symbol above or next to the place in the student's writing where the problem occurs. The student, knowing what it means, makes the necessary adjustment to his or her writing.

In order for students to benefit from the use of symbols such as these, they need to be trained in their use, as we shall see on pages 118–119.

Reformulation

Reformulation is a way of showing students how they could write something more correctly. Instead of asking them to find the mistake and correct it, the teacher shows how he or she would write the incorrect sentence. The student then learns by comparing correct and incorrect versions. Reformulation is extremely useful during drafting and re-drafting.

Referring students to a dictionary or a grammar book

Sometimes teachers indicate that a mistake has been made and then tell students to go and look the problem up in a dictionary or a grammar book. If, for example, the student writes *I am not interested about sailing*, the teacher can say 'Have a look at *interested* in your dictionary'. In the same way we can suggest that students consult a grammar book if they are having tense, grammar, or word order problems. (For an example of material for training students to use a dictionary successfully in this way, see page 120.)

The advantage of referring students to books in this way is that it encourages them to look at the information with a purpose in mind. They will learn as they correct.

Ask me

Sometimes it is difficult to explain a mistake on paper, or it is impossible to understand exactly what it was the student wanted to write. In such cases teachers can ask students to talk to them so that they can sort out the problem face-to-face.

Remedial teaching

When teachers read students' written work and they come across mistakes which many people in the same class are making, remedial teaching will then be necessary. In such cases, correction can be effected by showing the whole class sentences produced by the students that exemplify the mistake and asking them to help to put them right. It is a good idea for the example mistakes to be anonymous so that no individual student feels held up to ridicule.

Ways of responding to students' work

All the examples in the previous section have been concerned with the correct use of language. Correction has been applied to issues of grammar and lexis rather than to text design or issues of content.

Many students value this kind of correction extremely highly and feel uncomfortable when other kinds of feedback are offered. Yet, if we want to respond to written work as an assistant or a guide (rather than as an evaluator or judge), for example, a focus on only lexical and grammatical mistakes will not be appropriate. Responding to our students' work is about reacting to their ideas and to how they put them across.

Responding to work-in-progress

When students are involved in a writing task in class – especially where this is part of a process sequence – teachers will often 'visit' students and talk to them about what they are writing. We may ask what a certain sentence means, or wonder why they have started a composition in a particular way, or suggest that they re-check some information they have made notes about.

When, as teachers, we are involved with work-in-progress we have to think carefully about the way we give advice or make suggestions. It is very easy to say 'I wouldn't do it like that, I would do it like this', which, because it comes from the teacher, is taken by the student to be more or less a command. Sometimes there may be good reasons for this, and students may be very happy to receive such comments. Nevertheless, it is sometimes preferable to ask questions such as 'Why have you done it this way?' (asked as neutrally as possible) or 'What do you want the reader to understand here?', so that students have to come to their own decisions about how to revise and edit their work.

Students often get tremendous benefit from this kind of personal attention from teachers. For our part, we need to approach the task with great sensitivity, doing our best to draw decisions from the students themselves rather than telling them what to do.

However, not all students appreciate a teacher's intervention at any stage of the writing process. Sometimes, therefore, students should be allowed to leave a sign on their desk indicating whether or not they wish the teacher to help them. A piece of paper with a cross, the words *no, thanks*, or some other symbol will tell the teacher that for the moment the student wants to work on their own. A tick or *yes, please* obviously means the opposite.

If the class is taking place in a computer lab – where students are writing individually or in pairs – the teacher can look at their work on his or her screen, and either speak to the student (using a microphone and headset), or use an editing tool such as 'Track Changes' (see page 114).

Responding by written comment

Sometimes our response is delivered in written form when students hand us a draft of what they are working on. In such circumstances, it is always a good idea to write down what we think is good in the students' work. No one appreciates empty compliments, but encouragement is extremely important at this stage.

If students have written compositions about their childhood memories (see Example 4 on page 98), we may ask to see a draft version before they produce a final essay. Here it will be vital to be encouraging and helpful rather than judgmental. The teacher might write comments such as these:

> I enjoyed your draft composition very much. I liked the description of your grandparents. They sound like interesting people. In some ways they are the most interesting part of your story.
>
> I have one or two suggestions to make:
> - How about starting the composition with that description of your grandparents' house? It would be a good way in to the topic.
> - I wouldn't include the bit about your sister and the dog. It gets in the way of your story.
> - Be careful with your use of past tense verbs. Check whether you should use the past simple (I ran) or the past continuous (I was running).

Written responses to a student's work

Such advice can be extremely useful and should help students to avoid mistakes in their final version. It will almost certainly be constructed more effectively than it would have been without the teacher's intervention. Nevertheless, as with feedback on work-in-progress, these statements from the teacher may look more like commands and may close down the students' thinking rather than encouraging it. We could instead put most of our comments in question form to overcome this, for example: 'Which part of your story would be the best way to begin your composition, do you think? How important is the incident with your sister and the dog?'

Post-task statements

At the end of a writing sequence, however long or short, teachers usually end up giving final comments. While working at a Japanese university James Muncie wondered how to make this feedback situation useful in the development of his students' writing ability, instead of being only a final evaluation. His solution is to have students write 'future' statements based on the teacher's feedback and the processes which the drafting has gone through. At the end of each assignment, therefore, they write about 'how I can improve in future writing assignments', thus taking the experience forward into forthcoming writing tasks and activities.

Taped comments

If teachers cannot give face-to-face feedback they might well consider taping their comments about a piece of student writing on tapes provided by the students. This has the advantage (for some) of allowing them to be more expansive than written responses sometimes are. Students may well enjoy getting reactions in this format since it is both more personal and more immediate than written comments at the end of a paper.

Electronic comments

A lot of feedback can now be given electronically, either via e-mail or through text editing programmes. For the growing number of students who have access to computers and do their writing via a keyboard, feedback of this kind is extremely useful.

E-mailing comments to students is an ideal way of responding to their work as it goes through various drafts, since as students work at their computers they can incorporate the comments that their tutor is making, or reply to questions that are being asked. However, teachers need to lay down guidelines here, since, without them, there is the danger that students will e-mail them every time they have a new idea, and their lives could be completely taken over by such e-mail traffic.

Text editing packages, such as the 'Track Changes' tool that comes with Microsoft's Word application, allow teachers or other responders to make amendments and corrections, and also to leave notes and questions on a word-processed document which the student can react to at the same time as they edit that document on the screen. Once 'Track Changes' is engaged, students can either accept or reject the amendments that the teacher or

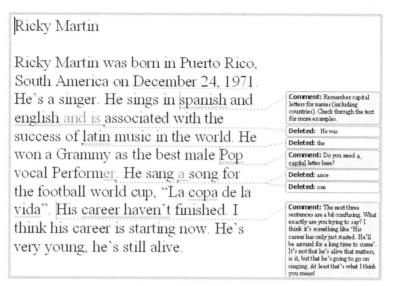

fellow student has suggested, and look, too, at the notes that have been attached to the document (see above).

A problem with this approach is that it can easily lead to the kind of over-marking we criticised on page 110. But if the relationship between teacher and student is one of sufficient trust, then the level of intrusion shown above should be acceptable.

As with all responding and correcting, teachers need to think carefully about what it is they want their students to understand as a result of the teacher's intervention. In the case of correction, we may just want to draw their attention, for example, to the fact that a tense has been misused, but at other times we may want to suggest that they should think a bit more carefully about what it is they want to say and how best to say it (as where the student above says *he's still alive*). We may want to tell them that while what they have said is perfectly correct, it doesn't express what they mean, or is said too inelegantly or idiosyncratically.

However, electronic comment and correction of this type differs from handwritten marking in one significant way − namely that it can be acted on instantly without the student having to find a fresh sheet of paper, rub things out, or make clean copies, etc. A click of the mouse accepts or rejects the changes. Typing is immediately 'clean', and a piece of correct writing can emerge within a very short space of time.

Peer review

Peer review is a valuable element in the writing process. It has the advantage of encouraging students to work collaboratively, something which, in a group, we want to foster. It also gets round the problem of students reacting too passively to teacher responses. As we have seen, it is sometimes difficult for students to see such responses from their teacher as anything other than commands which have to be obeyed. This reduces their self-reliance in the editing process. Although there are occasions where teacher correction and feedback may be extremely useful, still we want to develop our students' ability to edit and revise when they are on their own.

Peer review, therefore, is less authoritarian than teacher review, and helps students to view both colleagues and teachers as collaborators rather than evaluators. However, in order for it to be successful (especially when first introduced), students will need guidance from their teacher so that they know what to look at when they read their classmates' work.

When we ask our students to work on a new writing task, we may start by getting them to read an example in the same genre, or we may start by encouraging them to generate ideas and plans. In both cases, as we saw in Chapter 6, we will discuss what we can expect from a successful piece of writing, whether it is a report on traffic conditions, a biographical entry, a composition about 'my childhood', or a leaflet advertising a health centre. When we ask students to look at each other's drafts, therefore, we can refer them back to these discussions, so that they know what they are looking for. We can elicit from the students questions they might consider such as: 'Does the composition start in an interesting way? Is the story easy to follow?' They can look at each other's work to answer questions such as: 'Is the writing easy to understand?' or 'Is the writer's viewpoint clear?' Perhaps they could ask each other whether the language in the writing has the right level of formality, or whether enough information is given about the topic. These questions help to make peer review focused and productive. Without them, especially when students first start responding to each other's work in this way, the task may appear too amorphous for them to get to grips with.

When Victoria Chan organised a newspaper project with her class, she asked her students to consider the newspaper articles that their colleagues had written (as part of the project) in the ways we have described. She also gave them a comment form to guide them in their work:

From 'The Newspaper Project' by Victoria Chan in *Modern English Teacher*

Comment form

When reading your classmates' texts, you could also tell them your responses to the following points:

My immediate reactions to this piece of writing are ......
I find the content ......
I like the part on ......
The part on ...... could be further developed/elaborated.
You tend to ......
I'm not sure about ......
The specific language errors that I have noticed are ......
The best part of this writing is ......

Also, give suggestions on areas that need to be improved.

Although this looks highly prescriptive, nevertheless it gives student reviewers some clear points to consider, and shows how both positive and less positive comments can be useful for the editing process.

Peer review is not problem-free, however. In the first place, some students who rely on the teacher's approval may resent it, valuing their colleagues' opinions much less than their teacher's. Secondly, not all students work well together; the success of peer review may depend on exactly who is the reviewer and whose work is being reviewed. Finally, if students are not focused on the task, the quality of the feedback they have to offer may be questionable. Nevertheless, despite these dangers, getting students to help each other in the editing process can be extremely useful when handled in a sensitive and encouraging way.

Training students to self-edit and self-correct

If we want students to be able to edit their work based on teacher or peer review, or if we want them to be able to make corrections based on symbols, they need to know how to do this. Unless they know what the symbols mean, for example, the symbols won't be much use. Unless they believe in the editing process – and have some experience of it – they will not get sufficient benefit from this element of the writing process. We need, therefore, to train them to read their own work critically so that they can make corrections and changes with or without our guidance.

Finding mistakes

The first thing we need to do, when training students to edit their own work, is to enable them to notice mistakes. We can start this by putting incorrect sentences up on the board. Students come up and underline where they think the mistakes are, as here:

> I don't enjoy <u>to go</u> to the cinema.
> He lik<u>e</u> reading.
> Reading is <u>more better</u> than watching TV.

Later we can increase the sophistication of the task by giving students a mix of correct and incorrect sentences. They have to identify the sentences which have mistakes in them, for example:

> **Which of the following statements and questions are correct? Put a tick or a cross in the brackets.**
>
> a She likes watching television. [ ]
> b He hates playing football. [ ]
> c She enjoys to play tennis. [ ]
> d She is taller than her brother. [ ]
> e Her brother is not as tall than her. [ ]

Understanding correction symbols

If we want to use the kinds of correction symbols described on page 111, students need to be familiar with them. We can foster this using a three-stage technique:

- **Stage 1** – the teacher explains that the class is going to look at symbols which indicate mistakes and then puts the symbols, one by one, up on the board. The students guess what the symbols mean before the teacher makes things clear by showing examples. If the symbol *P* has been put on the board, for example, the teacher might write up the following:

> i live in new york   what's your name,

By having their attention drawn by the teacher to the *i*, the *n* of *new*, and the *y* of *york*, the students are made aware of the capital letter deficit. In the same way they understand that a question mark is needed (rather than a comma) in the question.

- **Stage 2** – the teacher can copy a piece of student work onto the board, or (better still) photocopy it, or type and print it on an overhead transparency (OHT). Photocopies or OHTs are then given to students who have to find the mistakes and write correction symbols beside them. Alternatively, students can come up to the board and write their symbols on the sentences the teacher has written there.

  If students have used marker pens to write symbols on an OHT, the teacher can project the transparency and discuss whether the symbols have been used correctly. Here is an example of how one group marked a **story circle** text (see page 79):

> Sp
> Once upon a time a beautif princess lived in a castle by a river.
> She was very clever.
> She always read and studied.
> T/ww   sp
> However she hasn't seen the gergous nature around her, where she
> was living,
> sp   T
> she had a stemother that hate her very much.
> She had a lovely dog.
> It was very loyalty. Gr
> One day, her stepmother bought a basket of red apples from the local
> market.
> ww
> The stepmother putted poison in apples.
> Her dog saw what the stepmother do, so, when the stepmother gave the
> ww   T   P
> apple to her, her dog jumped and ate the apple. Then, the dog died.

Student correction symbols on a typed OHT

The students can then discuss with their teacher whether the symbols have been used correctly (see, for example, 'ww' in the penultimate line), and the teacher can point out any mistakes that have been missed.

- **Stage 3** – the teacher hands the students some incorrect sentences with symbols included. The students have to identify the type of mistake (based on the symbols) and then write the sentences correctly.

Removing symbols gradually

Once students have become accustomed to the use of symbols – and to the idea that they will make corrections on their own when mistakes are indicated – teachers may want to gradually remove the help they give so that students are forced to do more of the correcting work themselves. This can occur in a number of stages:

- **Stage 1: Lines and symbols** – the teacher underlines the mistake and includes the symbol.

- **Stage 2: Underlining with no symbol** – the teacher underlines the place where the mistake occurs. The student has to work out what the mistake is.

- **Stage 3: Margin symbol** – the teacher writes the appropriate correction symbol in the margin next to the line where the mistake occurs. The student has to find out where the problem occurs and correct it.

- **Stage 4: Margin marks** – instead of using symbols, the teacher puts a mark (e.g. a cross) in the margin next to a line for every mistake there is in that line.

- **Stage 5: One margin mark** – the teacher puts a mark (e.g. a cross) in the margin next to the line, but does not say how many mistakes there are in the line. The student has to work it out.

Making corrections

When students are given back work, such as homework or drafts where their errors have been highlighted, it is a good idea if they are given time in class to rewrite the material correctly. However, it may be necessary to give them training exercises to develop their skills in correcting their work effectively. The activity on page 120 is an example of such an exercise, which is designed for dictionary training; it shows students how they can consult a dictionary (in this case) or a grammar book to help them make corrections.

It is worth repeating exercises like this from time to time to remind students how important it is to recognise and correct their mistakes, and how, each time they do this, it helps them to improve and learn more about writing in English.

A. Look at this piece of student homework.
The teacher has underlined some mistakes.
What was the student's mistake in each case?
Choose one of the following:

a) The student used the wrong word.

b) The student used language that was too informal, or
spoken rather than written English.

c) The student used the wrong adverb or preposition after
a verb.

For example, the word **chap** in the first line is too informal.
(*Answer:* **b**).

I used to know a chap called John who decided to
leave school when he was only fourteen. He was more
interested at money than work so he decided to rob
cars. The only problem was that he worked at a snail's
speed and so before long he was arrested and taken to
court. He was charged with pinching a car without the
owner's consent.
At his trial he pleaded good. He said he was only
making a joke on people, but he was found guilty. The
judge said she was appalled with the growth in childish
crime and so she was going to do an example of John.
She sentenced him for six years in prison.
In prison John started to study, and now he's a
university professor. End of story.

B. Looking at your dictionary when you need it, correct the
student's mistakes.

'Check and check again' from the Teacher's Resource Pack to accompany the *Longman Dictionary of Contemporary English*

Error checklist

Some teachers give their students an **error checklist** for them to use when
reading through what they have written. A checklist can be constructed in
a very simple way, like this:

1   Subject–verb agreement: *he likes*, not ~~he like~~
2   Past simple or Present: *I saw him yesterday*, not ~~I have seen him yesterday~~

The teacher can change the error checklist depending on the particular
errors that the class has been making recently.

Error checklists encourage students to edit their writing with care. The
examples we have suggested have dealt with grammar, but we can equally
well give them checklists on text layout and construction:

> The first sentence of each paragraph should introduce the subject/topic of the paragraph.

or register checklists:

> Business letters need formal greetings and 'signings-off'.

Directed questions

An alternative to checklists is to give students a series of questions for them to consider when editing their writing. We have seen an example of this in Chapter 6 where the teacher who asked students to write about their childhood experiences asked them to consider questions such as: 'Is the beginning interesting? Does it make you want to read on? Does it prepare you for what is going to come next?' Similarly, students who are working on a formal letter can be given questions such as these:

> 1 Where have you written your address? Is it in the right place?
> 2 Where is the address of the person you are writing to? Is it in the right place?
> 3 Where have you put the date? How have you written it?
> 4 What greeting have you used, and how have you signed off at the end of the letter?
> 5 What have you put in the first paragraph of the letter? Will the person reading it understand what the letter is going to be about?

Directed questions for letter writing

Discussing writing

When training students to deal with comments and corrections, it is extremely helpful to discuss these issues with them, and to hear their suggestions about how comments and corrections can best be offered and about how they themselves should respond. They may have marked views of their own which, if we can tap into them, will help the process work more effectively and smoothly.

In her book *Writing*, Tricia Hedge provides an activity where students have to decide on the relative importance of certain aspects of essay writing and then (in question 3 on page 122) compare their conclusions with the teacher's own checklist, in order to arrive at a negotiated list of priorities for successful writing.

There is no reason why we need to stick to the list in Hedge's activity. We might want to include other criteria for e-mails or business letters, for

Marking compositions

1 What do you think is most important in compositions? Put these things in order of importance (number them 1–10)

- ❏ correct grammar
- ❏ length
- ❏ originality of ideas
- ❏ spelling
- ❏ punctuation
- ❏ neat handwriting
- ❏ a good range of vocabulary
- ❏ complex and well-structured sentences
- ❏ good organisation with introduction, body, and conclusion
- ❏ keeping to the title

2 Is there anything missing from the list?

3 Find out from your teacher whether his/her criteria are:

    a. the same as those listed here;

    b. the same as your own.

4 What kind of grading system do you think is best?

    a. double (– figure + a letter) for content and language;

    b. single – a percentage out of 10;

                 – a grade.

5 Now use the criteria and the grading system to mark your essay.

From *Writing* by Tricia Hedge

example. But whatever the details, such activities help to focus the students' minds on what good writing is and should be. Through discussion, they will have insights about the process which they might otherwise not have been aware of.

Making homework successful

Whether our students do the majority of their writing in class or as homework will depend both on the type of course we are teaching and on the number of hours a week that students are studying. In a general English course of only 3 hours a week, there may be little time for in-class writing, but the same will probably not be true on intensive programmes which train students for academic study. But even where students do some writing in class, we will also want them to do written homework assignments.

Homework is often seen as a rather unglamorous chore despite its obvious benefits. It is often less successful than it should be, partly because of the tasks that are set and also because of the attitude of both teacher and students. There are various ways of overcoming some of these problems.

Discussing homework issues

It is a good idea to discuss homework with students. There are various topics to talk about:

- **Why homework?** – it is worth talking with students about what homework is useful for. We can make the point that it is a time when they can study on their own, putting into practice things they have seen and learnt in class. It will help them to remember things, and to work out language and construction problems that have been puzzling them. It helps the teacher understand how well they are doing and to plan future teaching.

- **Homework load** – there is no point in setting homework that students won't or can't do because of their other commitments. Especially in a school or university setting where English is just one of the many subjects fighting for the students' attention, it is important to find out how much homework all the different teachers expect, and then get agreement from the students about how English can fit into this programme. Where students have other calls on their time, we need to discuss how much time they can realistically spend on homework. This does not mean that students should lay down the law on this subject; only that without their co-operation and agreement homework will never be very successful.

- **Appropriate homework tasks** – students will be convinced of the value of doing homework if the tasks are seen to be appropriate – or rather, if the students can see the point of doing the task. Although there is nothing wrong with saying 'do exercise G on page 26', students can sometimes think that this is not very valuable or carefully considered on the part of their teacher. They are much more likely to give time for an activity which seems useful and which fits into the activities they have been involved in.

  One way of ensuring student co-operation is to ask them what kind of tasks they think would be helpful. What topics interest them? What kind of writing would they most like practice in? Students are far more likely to complete tasks which they themselves have chosen than ones which have been imposed on them. Once again, however, we are not suggesting that the teacher has no input in such discussions. He or she may well influence the students' preferences for different kinds of homework.

- **Explain the marking criteria** – it will help students if they know what the marking criteria for the homework are going to be. If we tell them that we are going to look at text organisation in particular, the students will spend more time on text organisation than they might otherwise have done. We can encourage them to concentrate especially upon spelling by making it one of our criteria. By saying what we will look at we make the homework process transparent and fair.

  When homework is handed back to students they need to be given time to look at the comments and corrections that have been made so they can write correct versions of their work (or develop new drafts).

- **Punctuality and even-handedness** – it is impossible to force a student to hand in homework, although we can use all sorts of blandishments and pressure to try and get him or her to do so. Nevertheless, it will help greatly if we show that we expect homework to be handed in when we have asked for it (rather than saying or showing that it doesn't really matter very much), and the homework procedure will benefit greatly from prompt marking on the part of the teacher. Students become extremely demotivated when the homework that they have worked hard to produce is left unmarked for an unreasonable amount of time.

Conclusions   In this chapter we have:

- discussed the difference between correcting and responding.
- looked at a number of different approaches to correction, including the use of correction symbols.
- shown how reformulation, referring students to dictionaries and grammar books, and asking students to talk to the teacher can also be extremely useful correction methods.
- detailed a number of different ways of responding to students' work – including spoken and written comments, and getting students to write post-task statements for future use.
- looked at ways of responding electronically to students' work.
- discussed the value of peer review and shown how, with judicious direction, we can help to make it a profitable part of writing.
- looked at ways of training students to use and understand various forms of correction and to edit their work.
- discussed the importance of homework and shown how getting students' agreement to it, setting appropriate tasks, and returning work promptly can all help to make it a success.

Looking ahead

- In the final chapter we will look at how writing journals can help students as writers – and also as learners.

8 Journal writing

I write to find out what I'm talking about.
Edward Albee

- A different kind of writing
- Journal writing benefits
- Before, during, and after
- Teacher journals

A different kind of writing

Many teachers ask their students to write journals as a quite separate activity from the other kinds of writing they do in lessons or as homework. Such journal writing involves students in keeping their own 'diaries' in which they can write about a range of different topics such as significant recent events in their lives, how they are getting on in class, which language points they are having particular difficulty with, or, indeed, any other area of interest to them.

Although there are, as we shall see, a range of options available to teachers about how they should respond to their students' journals, it is generally the case that students are happy to have their writing read, and welcome feedback on it in some form or other.

In this chapter we will discuss the many good pedagogical and affective reasons for journal and letter writing. However, as will become apparent, in order for this kind of writing to be a success, teachers and students have to make decisions about how, when, and where to write (at home, in class, or in a study centre, for example). Students should also know when and how teachers will respond to their writing. Above all they must feel empowered by writing journals rather than seeing this task as yet another learning chore.

Journals and letters

Some teachers write to their students at the beginning of a term and invite the students to write letters back to them. As with journals, they can write about anything they want and the letters are kept confidential between them.

Many commentators speak about journals and letters as being equivalent in the context of teacher–student dialogue. However, there are some significant differences between them. In the first place, whereas journals encourage introspection and reflection because students are essentially writing to and for themselves (with an eye, of course, on the teacher's response if one is to be given), letters are written to someone (in this case the teacher). Letters may gain in dialogue power, in other words, but this may be at the expense of individual analysis.

In the second place, whereas it may be quite possible to ask students to write weekly journal entries, asking for weekly letters is less satisfactory. When teachers write to students they invite them to reply, but coercion is not part of the bargain. Journal writing is easy to consider as part of a learning and writing process, in other words, and can be a regular feature of lesson sequences whereas letter writing is, by its nature, a more voluntary procedure which is difficult to insist upon in the same way.

For these reasons journal writing is seen by some teachers as preferable to letter writing. Others, however, have found sending letters to students and getting ones back again a rewarding experience, both for themselves and, more importantly, for their students who, as we shall see on page 127, benefit enormously from an effective teacher–student dialogue.

In this chapter our principal focus will be on writing journals, but much of the discussion will be appropriate to teacher–student letter exchange as well.

Journal writing benefits

There are many reasons why teachers and their students have found journal and letter writing to be useful. These include not only the benefits of reflecting upon learning, but also the opportunities for freedom of expression, the impact of journal writing on writing ability in general, and the opportunity they provide for teachers and their students to enter into a new and different kind of dialogue.

The value of reflection

Journals provide an opportunity for students to think both about how they are learning (what is easier or more difficult, and why and how they achieve success), and also about what they are learning (aspects of the language and how it all fits together). This kind of introspection may well lead them to insights which will greatly enhance their progress.

When we try to put our thoughts into words we have to work out what those thoughts are. This, in turn, makes us reflect on what has happened, what we think or how we feel. And when we reflect on things we often reach conclusions that we might not have thought of when an event was taking place or when, as learners, we were engaged in the learning process itself.

A marked benefit of such creative introspection is its effect on memory. There are good reasons for supposing that when we have a chance to reflect carefully on what we have done we are far more likely to remember it than if we simply discard an experience the moment it is over.

Freedom of expression

Journals allow students to express feelings more freely than they might do in public, in class. If they know that their journals are not going to be read by everyone (unless they want people to read them), they will write more openly. And because the act of writing is less immediate than spontaneous conversation, they have more time to access those feelings.

Such freedom of expression is in contrast to some of the other types of writing which students are called upon to produce. When writing within certain genres ('letters', 'reports', 'narratives', etc.) they are sometimes constrained by what is appropriate within those genres and by what they are trying to learn to do. Such writing will often be corrected and evaluated, and may or may not lead to passing or failing grades.

Journal writing is a genre in its own right, of course, but within that genre authors are at liberty to impose their own idiosyncratic style on the writing since their primary audience is, after all, themselves. They can decide what and how much they want to include, and they can write at their own speed.

Developing writing skills

Just as reading a lot helps students to become better readers, so the more students write, the better and more fluent they become as writers. They expand their range of written expression and write with greater ease and speed. Journal writing contributes to a student's general writing improvement in the same way as training enhances an athlete's performance: it makes them fit.

If journal writing is successfully encouraged – and if the conditions for journal writing are appropriate – it has a powerful effect upon their motivation too, quite apart from promoting learner autonomy in writing.

Student–teacher dialogue

One of the merits of journal (and letter) writing is the dialogue it encourages between teacher and students. When a teacher writes to a class and says, 'you can write to me on any subject and I will reply. But do not worry, I will not show your letter to anybody else, and you do not have to write to me if you do not want to', the student knows they have a channel of communication that was not there before. When a student writes in a journal, he or she knows that the teacher will read what is written with, perhaps, a different eye from the normal evaluative one. A different kind of conversation therefore takes place.

A confidential channel of communication between teacher and student can cause problems both of time pressure and of the erosion of 'distance' between them (two areas of concern that are discussed on page 133). However, it is noticeable that students more readily 'open up' in this medium than in others.

Student journals are an extremely useful resource for teachers, too. They frequently trigger insights into the effect of classroom methodology. When students say how they feel about things, teachers often find responses to lesson segments that they had not anticipated. Learner perceptions are often different from teacher perceptions.

When we find things in student journals that we did not expect, we can make changes or introduce elements that answer our students' concerns. When Lakshmy Krishnan and Lee Hwee Hoon asked students to keep diaries at the Nanyang Technological University in Singapore they found themselves 'listening' to 'voices' which gave them strong messages about individual concerns and needs. Their students were attending a pre-semester, intensive English language course. They were mostly Indonesians and Malaysians and they were new to Singapore and its culture.

What quickly became clear from their journals was that many of them felt uneasy about being in a new place, about having to make new relationships, and about having to do things differently. One student wrote: *I should go to bed now for getting up on time and I won't be late for tomorrow's class in the computer lab. I think my roommate and I have to go out earlier because we should find the lab first. I'm afraid I'll be lost, like today I lost when I tried to find the canteen. Although I've already the map and asked people. Finally I still can't find it, so I come back to my hall.* Another student wrote: *I feel homesick because I usually spend my time with my family but I hope I can handle it.*

Neither of these entries is especially surprising, but as teachers we sometimes forget what it is like for students when they first arrive in a new place far away from home. At the Nanyang Technological University in Singapore, these journal entries encouraged the course leaders to think of ways to help students. Perhaps they could institute a 'buddy' system to prevent student loneliness; next time they might design a 'treasure hunt' which would teach students how to get around the campus. Other entries told them about students' attitudes to different classroom activities and suggested areas for amendments to teaching practices.

When we read our students' journals we can respond in writing to their questions and concerns, making suggestions, offering advice, and empathising with them. But however we respond to what we read, we know things that we might not have known before, and therefore have a chance to act on them.

Before, during, and after

For journal writing to be a success, teachers and students have to know what it is for and be enthusiastic about the process. This means that a number of strategies have to be adopted and a number of potential pitfalls avoided.

Starting out

Although some of our students may well have kept diaries when they were younger (and a few may still do this), most of them will never have contemplated keeping a journal in their own first language. The idea of keeping an English-language journal, therefore, is doubly strange. Such students are unlikely to become instant journal writers just because we ask them to. Unless they are encouraged, helped, and supported as journal writers, they will probably be reluctant to take part.

There are three main things that we can do to make journal writing a success:

- **Be enthusiastic** – the first thing students need to perceive is that their teacher is really enthusiastic about the idea of journal writing. We need to be able to show by the way we talk about it that we are really keen on the idea and that we think it will be both fun and useful. If students pick up on our enthusiasm, they might just become inspired by it.

- **Explain why and what** – we need to tell students why we are asking them to write journals. We need to impress on them our belief that journal writing is good – as we have seen above – for learning (because it gives us time to reflect on what we have been studying), good for writing (because the more we practise, the better we become), good for flexing our creative muscles (because we have the freedom to experiment with different forms of expression), and good for being able to communicate with the teacher.

When students have understood why we are suggesting they should write journals, we need to talk about the kind of writing they might do. We may explain that they can write about any difficulties they have with the language or with the lessons; they can write about any interesting things that have happened to them – and which they want to talk about; they can discuss any issues that concern, interest, or amuse them. At this point we may show them a number of different journal entries, either ones produced by previous students (with those students' permission) or concocted ones, for use as examples of what might be done.

We then need to tell them what they can expect from us. We will tell them if and how we are going to respond to what they write and how often we are going to do this (we will discuss these issues below).

- **What kind of journal/notebook?** – some teachers issue all their students with the same kind of notebook. Other teachers tell students to go and choose whatever kind of notebook they want. If we take the latter course, we must insist that students come to class with their new journals at the appointed time so they can start writing along with everyone else. However, there will always be at least one or two students who forget to buy a decent notebook, and so we may want to have some spares in reserve.

  Discussion of what kind of notebook students should have may seem trivial, but the decision we take might help to make the difference between enthusiastic and non-enthusiastic students. However, we will need to measure the desirability of having students write in the kind of notebooks they like against the disadvantage (for the teacher) of having to carry around notebooks of all different shapes and sizes.

- **How often and when?** – there is no hard and fast rule about how often and when students should write their journals or send letters to their teacher. Ideally, they will want to do this as often as they can. However, as with any other student-determined activity, there will be big differences between those who are committed and able to take action on their own and those who, for whatever reason, find it less easy to work by and for themselves. Yet if we believe that journal writing is a useful activity for the reasons we have been discussing, then we want as many students as possible to take part.

  It is for this reason that many teachers who get their students to write journals set aside a few minutes, say at the end of the week, to give their students in-class writing time. Sometimes teachers like to play appropriate music in the background to create a 'journal-writing atmosphere'. Not all students like writing (or working) to music, however, so it is a good idea to ask the class if they would like this, and what kind of music they would appreciate if they have agreed.

Getting students to write journals in class has the disadvantage of taking time from other activities. Nevertheless, five or ten minutes at the end of a week or fortnight may be very beneficial for the students' language and writing skills.

With journal writing there is always a conflict between, on the one hand, trying to ensure that it takes place (which suggests in-class writing, and the handing in of journals every week or fortnight for reading) and, on the other, giving the students space and freedom to use journals for reflection and personal development (which suggests allowing them to decide when and where they want to write them). This may be resolved by, as we have suggested, starting a journal-writing programme and asking to see students' work at set intervals. As journal writing takes hold, these formally scheduled events can be reduced until it is up to the students to decide when to write. Teachers can then concentrate on those who seem to have stopped their journals. They can ask them why they have done so and encourage them to start again.

The question of how often to have students write journals is connected to one of the problems of journal and letter writing, namely the danger of imposing an impossible workload on the teacher (see page 132).

Keeping going

As with many techniques and activities in class, it is significantly easier to get students started than to maintain their enthusiasm over a long period of time. But journal writing is, by its nature, an ongoing procedure rather than a one-off classroom activity. We need to do everything we can, therefore, to maintain our students' interest, motivation, and participation.

- **Making it work** – to make sure that journal writing works, we must continue to show enthusiasm for the project and, if appropriate, give some class time to journal writing (see above). We also need to respond to our students when we have said we will and in the way that we and the students have agreed on.

- **Responding to journals** – there are many different ways of responding to students' journals, and the one we choose may well determine the success or failure of the whole journal-writing enterprise. It is quite possible to argue, for example, that student journals should remain entirely private so that neither the teacher nor any of a student's classmates should see what he or she has written. This would give the journal keeper real space in which to be creative and address his or her inner thoughts with a feeling of confidence and safety. In this case the teacher's role would be to repeatedly encourage the students to keep on with their journals. The students might discuss the merit of their journals and how they were getting on with them without having to show the actual writing itself.

  Another alternative, however, is for teachers to read what students are writing in their journals, so that, as we have seen earlier in this chapter, the journal becomes a channel for a different kind of student–teacher dialogue. However, this raises the question of what teachers do with what they read. One possibility would be for the teacher to read the journals without making any comment at all. At least, then, students know that the teacher has seen what they have to say. But the dialogue will be somewhat one-sided.

Perhaps, then, we should respond in some way to what we are reading. Once again, however, we have to decide exactly what form this response should take. We could, for example, write a comment at the end of a journal entry which showed that we had read what the student had written. For example, we might write, 'I enjoyed reading your journal this week. Well done', which is a supportive comment but not very informative. Perhaps, instead, we could say, 'I liked your description of the party you went to. It sounds like it was fun'. This at least shows students that you have read and absorbed some of what they have written. Perhaps our response could include a comment like, 'Be careful about *since* and *for*. We use *for* with a period of time (*three weeks*, *two hours*, etc.) and *since* with an actual time (*1999*, *six o'clock*, etc.)'. This shows that we are paying attention to the students' English as well as to the content of what they are writing about. Of course we can go further than this and underline the mistakes in the students' writing in the same way as we correct some of their written homework, for example.

In general it seems that journal writing naturally provokes the kind of responses (rather than correction) that were discussed in Chapter 7. If we are asking students to be reflective about their learning or to offer us their thoughts on a range of subjects, it seems churlish and demotivating to respond with a long list of corrections. Nevertheless some students do appreciate help with their English, even in this kind of writing.

Perhaps the way of resolving this kind of dilemma is to ask classes what kind of response they would like. That's what Richard Watson Todd and his colleagues in Thailand did with their students. What was clear to them was that the students wanted feedback from the teachers who read their journals, provided that trust was established between them and the teacher. It was in this way that appropriate dialogue was established and maintained. But when asked, students made it clear that for them a general comment at the end of a journal entry was not enough. They wanted in-text feedback when the teacher had something to say (the same could be achieved, of course, with footnotes). In other words, these journal writers wanted comments at the place in the text where the teacher had concerns or other reactions. The comments that the students most valued were suggestions, positive evaluation, or supportive back-up. Another message seemed to be that tutors did not have to worry too much about what they commented on; all comments on specific points were appreciated.

The findings of Watson Todd and his colleagues may be specific to the group of learners in their study. Nevertheless, two things emerge from what was discovered. Firstly, the best feedback to give on learner journals is feedback that both teacher and students feel confident about, and which students find helpful. And the best way to find out what kind of feedback this is, is to ask them about it. We can say, for example, that though we are not especially concerned with grammatical accuracy in the journals, we will point out errors if the students want it, but not if they don't. We can ask them if they want us to write in-text comments as and when there is something to comment on. As the journal writing progresses, we can ask them again if they are happy with the feedback they are getting (we can ask this by writing the questions in their journals) and amend our feedback on the basis of their replies.

We have been talking as if asking students for their opinions is something that only happens between teachers and classes. But in fact there are good reasons for suggesting that we should be asking individual students for their opinions rather than relying on the opinions of a whole group. There are two reasons for this: in the first place, a group 'consensus' may not in fact represent the wishes of all the individuals within the group. Different students may have different needs and wishes and would benefit, individually, from markedly different kinds of feedback. Secondly, it is often difficult to hear individual points of view when we ask groups for their opinions. There is always the danger that those with 'louder' voices will be heard more clearly than others and thus seem to represent a group's wishes, even if this is not strictly true. What is being suggested is that, as well as discussing feedback issues with the group, we should also ask individual students if they are comfortable with the level and type of feedback that they are receiving.

A general principle of journal writing is that, because it offers a different kind of writing and a different mode of communication, it should not be treated in the same way as other kinds of student writing. However, the exact nature of the feedback we give will emerge as a result of the students' comments and replies to us.

- **When to respond** – one of the dangers of writing letters to students and inviting them to write back to you is that they might all do just that! If a teacher is working with five groups of 30 students each – a common situation in many parts of the world – the danger is that he or she will be having to answer 150 letters a week. This is somewhat unlikely, of course, but the danger of serious teacher overload should not be underestimated.

As with letters, so with journals. No teacher could reply adequately to 150 journal entries a week on top of lesson preparation, classroom teaching, and homework marking. Some way, therefore, has to be found to cut down on the teacher's workload while, at the same time, maintaining the benefits of teacher–student dialogue.

Not all of a teacher's groups may keep journals, of course. A lot depends on the level of the students and the type and make-up of the group. The amount that individual students write will also affect how often we can respond to their journals. But even where teachers have a large number of students writing journals, there are ways of working with the situation. We can, for example, make 'appointments' to read an individual's journal. Instead of reading it every week, we might say we will read it twice a term, and say when that will be. We could read one group's journals one week, and another group's the next. We can ask students to restrict themselves to writing no more than one or two pages (though it may be unfortunate to curtail students' expressivity in this way).

- **The teacher–student relationship** – we have advocated the use of journal (and letter) writing to promote a teacher–student dialogue. However, as teachers we always have to be careful about the relationship such dialogue engenders. At its best it is extremely creative and a powerful force in both the student's development as a learner and the teacher's understanding of how students think and respond. However, it can, very occasionally, become difficult if students express opinions (whether personal, social, or political) which the teacher finds questionable or objectionable.

  As teachers we need to remember that journal-writing dialogue, like any other form of communication with students, is a professional issue, and the relationship that such dialogue creates is a professional relationship. In other words, where things become difficult, teachers need to make clear to students as soon as possible the limits of such dialogue. These do not include, for example, a student's right to make abusive journal entries or include views which in any other context would be unacceptable. The privacy of a journal is not a cover for inappropriate communication.

  Where journals and letters cause difficulties in this way we need, in the first instance, to speak to the student and explain the problem. We may, then, make our feelings known very directly in our responses to journals. Finally, we may find it necessary to suspend our reading of that student's journal or letters either temporarily or permanently.

  Such problems are rare. But teachers need to be aware of the possibility of difficulties like this, so they can quickly spot them and take action immediately before things get out of hand.

Teacher journals

In this chapter we have focused on student journals (and letters) and the teacher's response to them. However, teachers can and do write journals as well, with some or all of the same benefits as those they have for students.

Reflective journals

Many teachers keep journals in which they record their thoughts about their teaching and their students. Just as a student journal is a powerful reflective device which allows them to use introspection to make sense of their experience, so teacher journals allow them to make sense of classroom experience in the same way.

Teacher journals are powerful **action research** tools. Action research is the term used to describe the ways in which we look at our classroom practice – and its success or failure – with a critical and evaluative eye. Thus a teacher may worry, for example, about the fact that students do not write fluently in lessons. In such a situation, he or she can think of different ways of trying to improve the situation, and can introduce a series of different activities over a period of time which might get students writing more effectively. By keeping a journal and recording the responses to each of these activities, the teacher – like any observational scientist – has something to refer back to when coming to conclusions about the best way to proceed in the future.

It is not being suggested that keeping a journal is the only way to conduct action research. On the contrary, teachers can use a variety of other techniques such as questionnaires (to students), various observational tools (including having lessons videotaped to watch them later), or peer teaching (where colleagues collaborate in teaching and observing each other's lessons). But journal keeping has a unique power to provoke creative introspection which may sometimes solve problems that otherwise seem intractable.

Teacher-to-student journals

Teachers can write journals at the same time as their students, of course, and students can respond to them just as teachers respond to their work. A teacher–student journal swap will have an enormous impact and help to create trust and an equal dialogue. Students may well be just as interested in the teacher's introspection as they are in their own reflective thoughts.

However, such a swap could cause massive overload problems for the teacher of the kind we discussed above. A more realistic option might be to publish a teacher journal/newsletter which is distributed to the whole class with the same regularity as we are asking students to make entries in their own journals.

Another possibility is to select a different student each week. It would be their responsibility to read the teacher's journal and then report back to the class about what they find there. This gives the individual student a very positive responsibility, and may lead to energetic discussion between the student, the teacher, and the group.

Because it is important to create and maintain an appropriate teacher–student relationship, we need to take care with what we put in such journals and newsletters. We should probably not engage in too public an introspection about the progress of the class, precisely because we are writing for the public, and not just for ourselves or one other person. We should also take care that we don't write anything which could be hurtful, misconstrued, or upset the balance of fairness and equal treatment that we, as teachers, attempt to create in our classes.

Many teachers will feel that the responses they give to their students' journals constitute a kind of journal in themselves. Nevertheless, for some students and teachers a journal written by the teacher and read by the students helps to encourage them to write their own journals for the teacher to read.

Conclusions

In this chapter we have:
- discussed the advantages of having students write journals, and contrasted journal and letter writing.
- said that introspection and reflection help people become better learners.

- pointed out that journal writing is good for both language and writing improvement.
- explained how student journal writing and appropriate teacher response create a unique kind of teacher–student dialogue.
- said that teachers will need to encourage students to write.
- talked about how often and where students should write journals.
- pointed out that teachers need to help students with their writing, and continue to motivate them, especially by the way they respond to their students' journals.
- discussed the nature of the teacher's response, saying that it helps to ask students how they want us to respond.
- made it clear that teachers have to maintain a professional relationship with their students and act immediately where this appears problematic.
- discussed the usefulness of teacher journals both as reflective tools for ourselves and as models and motivators for our students.

Task File

Introduction

- The exercises in this section all relate to topics discussed in the chapter to which the exercises refer. Some expect definite answers, while others only ask for the reader's ideas and opinions.
- Tutors can decide when it is appropriate to use the tasks in this section. Readers on their own can work on the tasks at any stage in their reading of the book.
- An answer key is provided after the Task File (on pages 145–147) for those tasks where it is possible to provide specific or suggested answers.
- The material in the Task File can be photocopied for use in limited circumstances. Please see the note on the back of the title page for photocopying restrictions.

**TASK FILE
Chapter
1**

Writing as a process

☞ **A How people write** Pages 4–6

Copy the **process wheel** from page 6 and then show (using arrows and numbers) the process that the writers went through in the following examples.

Process 1

After receiving an e-mail about the possibility of a meeting, she thought about how to reply. She typed in her answer and, on reading it through, found a couple of mistakes she wanted to put right. She was just about to hit the 'send' button when she changed her mind and changed some of the text of the e-mail. She read it through again and, satisfied, she sent the e-mail.

Process 2

For days he had been carrying the image in his brain. He let the words flow through his head so that when he came to write the story he did it at one sitting and sent it straight off to his publisher – who did not change one word of it.

Process 3

When they started thinking about the design of the brochure, they sat around and discussed what should go in it. Marion made some notes as they talked. Then she went away and wrote a version for the next meeting. Everyone read it and made suggestions. She went off and incorporated their comments and presented the final version to the next meeting. Just as she was about to send it off to be printed, the managing director rang her and said he thought they should discuss the brochure again. They had another discussion (this time with the managing director present) and she did another version, which she modified on the basis of further comments from her colleagues. Finally, she sent the brochure to the printers, breathing a huge sigh of relief.

☞ **B Writing and speaking** Pages 6–11

Are the following more likely to be characteristics of speaking (S) or of writing (W)? Put the appropriate letter in the brackets.
1 Condensed questions ( )
2 Contracted forms ( )
3 Error tolerance ( )
4 Face-to-face communication ( )
5 General audience ( )
6 Higher lexical density ( )
7 Higher proportion of grammatical words ( )
8 Non-clausal units ( )
9 Paralinguistic features ( )
10 Phrasal verbs ( )
11 Pressure for correctness ( )
12 Time-bound ( )

**TASK FILE
Chapter
2**

Describing written text

☞ **A Genre**   Pages 15–27

Analyse the following extracts in terms of genre, register, and topic vocabulary. What kind of writing do they represent? What register are they written in? What topic vocabulary makes this clear?

Extract 1
'Absolutely! (perhaps)'
Ensemble piece written by Luigi Pirandello and directed by Franco Zeffirelli, with Joan Plowright, Oliver Ford Davies, and Lisa Tarbuck.
Wyndham's Theatre, Charing Cross Road, WC2 (020-7639-1736) Mon–Sat 7.30 pm, mats Wed & Sat 2.30 pm to Aug 23, £15–£40.

Extract 2
Alarm for PM as union crown falls to left-winger.

Extract 3
Memory
whether you knock on it, split it
eat it, can't bear to eat it
there it sits on your table
thump-ripe
already spoiling

Extract 4
Thank you so much for a lovely Sunday. It was excellent to see you again and very relaxing. I hope you had a good time the rest of the holiday. We're back in Seville now but have been to lots of cute Andalucian towns – this one (Ronda) was amazing especially the Semana Santa processions. Glad to be going back though. Hope to see you in May. Lots of love.

Extract 5
The bodies were discovered at eight forty-five in the morning of Wednesday 18th September by Miss Emily Wharton, a 65-year-old spinster of the parish of St Matthew's in Paddington, London, and Darren Wilkes, aged 10, of no particular parish as far as he knew or cared.

Extract 6
Although other viruses may infect the liver as part of a wider infection, certain viruses attack the liver as their primary target. These include five named viruses, hepatitis viruses A, B, C, D, and E, in addition to some others that have not yet been identified. The hepatitis A and E viruses are transmitted mostly by the contamination of drinking water by infected faeces. The E virus is found mostly in developing countries, whereas the A virus is common throughout the world.

Extract 7
The ABS brake system makes itself noticeable through the pulsating of the brake pedal and the noise of the regulation process. Your vehicle is now in a critical situation; the ABS allows you to keep control of the vehicle and reminds you to match your speed to the road conditions.
  To achieve maximum braking, keep the brake pedal fully depressed throughout the braking process, despite the fact that the pedal is pulsating. Do not reduce pressure on the pedal.

Extract 8
The most obvious face of **tango** in Buenos Aires is that of the large tango *espectáculos* offered by places such as *El Viejo Almacén*. Often referred to by the Porteños as 'tango for export', these generally rather expensive shows are performed by professionals who put on a highly skilled and choreographed display. The shows can be dazzling, but if you want to dance yourself – or would prefer to see the tango as a social phenomenon – you'd be better off heading to one of the city's dancehalls to experience the popular *Milongas* (for more on these, see the box on p. 140).

TASK FILE
Chapter
3

Writing in the language classroom

☞ **A Writing for learning; writing for writing**   Pages 31–38

Look at the following exercises and say whether they are 'writing-for-learning' or 'writing-for-writing' activities. Are they good writing activities do you think?

Exercise 1

You have gone on a group holiday to a place that you have never been to before. You have just landed at the place. Write an e-mail to an English-speaking friend. Describe:
• the place   • the journey there
• what you think of the other people you are with   • how you feel at the moment.

Exercise 2

Imagine that you are planning a party to celebrate an event such as the end of a course, New Year's Eve, or an important birthday. You have unlimited money for your party.
a Decide where the party should be, when it should start, what music you want, what food and drink you want, and what will make your party one that people will remember.
b Write an invitation for the party you have decided to hold.

Exercise 3

Write six sentences about what you do every day using the present simple.

Exercise 4

You have been asked to write an article for your school magazine on the following question: 'What would your dream home be like?' Write your article in 120–180 words.

Exercise 5

Do you like shopping? Write four sentences about shopping using the following expressions.
• comfort shopping   • shopping spree
• supermarket shopping   • window-shopping

☞ **B Writing purposes**   Page 39

Read the descriptions and tick the most appropriate box for each one.

The students:	ESL	ESP	EFL
1 are learning for general language improvement.			
2 are learning in order to use English in the place they are living.			
3 are living in the target language community.			
4 are visiting the target language community.			
5 do writing tasks which most people would have to do whatever their occupation.			
6 do writing tasks which reflect their occupations (or the occupations they are studying for).			
7 have no specific or identifiable needs other than to learn the language as effectively as possible.			
8 have specific writing needs.			
9 are studying because they are going to do a particular job and need the language for that job.			

TASK FILE
Chapter
4

Nuts and bolts

A Sounds and spelling   Page 47

How could you divide the following words into two lists based on the sounds of the letter 'c'?

| cake | call | came | cat | catch | cell | cent | certain |

| cinema | city | coffee | coin | cost | could | cry | cup |

| custom | cycle | dance | decide | place | policy |

How would you use your lists to help students work out rules for the sounds of 'c'?

B Punctuation   Page 49

Look at the following extract from a story for students. How could you use it to give your students punctuation practice?

'Do you have a boyfriend in the orchestra?'
'That's a very personal question,' I said.
'Death is a very personal answer,' he said, very quietly.
'Yes. Sorry,' I said. I suddenly saw Frank's body again.
'So?' he asked.
'What?' I said.
'What's the answer? Do you have a boyfriend in the orchestra?'
'Yes,' I said.
'Who is that?'
'Simon Cheshunt,' I told him.
'And did he … did you spend the night together?' he asked.
'Well no, not actually,' I said. I wasn't enjoying this.
'I see.' He put his pen in his mouth. He didn't say anything for a moment. Then he looked into my eyes. 'All right,' he said, 'that's all.'
'You aren't going to ask me any more questions?' I asked. 'I can go?'
'Yes. For now,' he said, 'but don't go far. Nobody in the orchestra can leave Barcelona. Stay near the hotel.'
'Of course.'
'I'll talk to you again,' he said. He was smiling again. 'All right?'
'Oh yes,' I said, 'good.' But I didn't feel good at all.

C Sentence, paragraph, and text   Pages 55–59

What do you understand by **parallel writing**?
Write a paragraph about one of the following topics which the students can then imitate in similar ways to the examples in Chapter 4.
• Famous films or plays
• Famous paintings
• Famous people
• Famous pieces of music or songs
• Famous places or buildings.

TASK FILE Chapter 5

Building the writing habit

A Building confidence and enthusiasm   Pages 61–63

Match the teacher actions in the left-hand column with the reasons for doing them in the right-hand column.

Teacher's actions

1 Teachers can encourage students to read each other's work (or they can display it)
2 Teachers can use writing with clear formulaic patterns (such as poems, for example)
3 Teachers may want to have students move round the class or do something active
4 Teachers may want to use pictures
5 Teachers need to be ready to suggest ideas and language
6 Teachers should choose appropriate activities
7 Teachers should give the appropriate amount of clear information about the task
8 Teachers should not too readily assume that a possible activity is inappropriate
9 Teachers should try to engage their students

Teacher's reasons

a for those students who find instant (or any other kind of) writing difficult.
b so that students know exactly what they are expected to do.
c if they think their students respond well to kinaesthetic stimuli.
d so that students feel their writing is worth something.
e so that they are not just intellectually involved, but emotionally as well.
f because sometimes groups enjoy things we had not expected them to.
g if they want students to engage with the task.
h to help students follow a clear model and thus make the writing easier.
i with students who respond particularly well to visual stimuli.

B Sentence writing   Page 64

Choose two of the following topics. For each one you have chosen, write half-sentences for students to complete.

Eating out ....
Friendship ....
Homelessness ....
Modern music ....
Parties..

Shopping..
Sport..
Television...
Tourism..

C Using pictures   Pages 67–69

How many different writing activities can you think of which could be used with these pictures?

A

B

TASK FILE Chapter 6

'Worked-on' writing

☞ A Analysing genres
Page 91

Look at the film review and consider these questions:

- What level would you expect students to be, before they could read something like this?
- What genre-analysing questions would you ask them to consider when looking at reviews like this?
- How would you build a writing task around this text?

☞ B Project work   Page 103

What order would the following stages of a project go in?* Put them in the table.

- Briefing/choice
- Data gathering
- Drafting and editing
- Final version
- Idea/language generation
- Planning

Respiro

Philip French

Vincenzo Amato's *Respiro* received three prizes at Cannes last year. It has a plot frequently encountered in movies from Latin countries – the story of a beautiful woman in a backward, tradition-bound society who is turned into a pariah by lusting men and jealous women for her independent, wilful ways.

A recent example is Giuseppe Tornatore's *Malèna*, set in wartime Sicily and starring Monica Bellucci. Here the victim is Grazia (played by the gorgeous Valeria Golino who was Tom Cruise's girlfriend in *Rain Man*), a fisherman's impetuous, freewheeling wife on the impoverished, sun-drenched island of Lampedusa off the south-west coast of Sicily.

She's driven to madness and thoughts of suicide by her insensitive husband and his family who want to institutionalise her, and she turns to her 14-year-old son for help. It's beautiful to look at and Golino is immensely sympathetic. But it strains after a timeless mythic significance and ends up neither realistic nor poetic.

(from *The Observer*)

---

1 →	2 →	3 →	4 →	5 →	6

Choose a subject for a project. Say what level it is for, and then make notes in the chart about how the different stages could be achieved (e.g. what kind of data could be collected and how) and what your role as the teacher might be.

* Although drafting, planning, and the production of various versions (including the final version) are part of a complex interlocking pattern (described in the **process wheel** on page 6), in this exercise the sequence which might take place has been simplified/idealised.

**TASK FILE
Chapter
7**

Responding, correcting, and guiding

☞ **A** **Correcting and responding** Pages 108–110

Are the following actions or behaviour more likely to be examples of 'correcting' or 'responding'? Tick the appropriate column.

	Correcting	Responding
1 At the 'draft' stage, the teacher suggests changes in both content and (grammatical and lexical) form.		
2 The teacher asks a student to explain why he has written something in a certain way.		
3 The teacher tells a student to check a particular issue in a grammar book.		
4 The teacher is chiefly concerned with accuracy.		
5 The teacher is interested in content more than in accuracy.		
6 The teacher is performing the role of an examiner.		
7 The teacher is performing the role of an audience.		
8 The teacher marks the mistakes in a piece of 'writing for learning'.		
9 The teacher selects the kind of problems that are going to be highlighted when the students' work is handed back.		
10 The teacher tells a student how much she enjoyed their piece.		
11 The teacher uses symbols on a piece of homework to show where things have gone wrong.		
12 The teacher gives students advice to help them avoid the same mistakes in the future.		

☞ **B** **Homework** Pages 122–124

Rewrite the following sentences so they reflect your own opinion.

1 Homework is for reinforcing classwork.
2 It doesn't matter whether students hand in their homework on time.
3 Students don't mind waiting to get their homework back.
4 Students should do three pieces of written homework every week.
5 Teachers should always correct the mistakes in their students' homework.

Journal writing

☞ **A Journals and letters** Pages 125–126

Copy and complete the table with advantages and disadvantages of having students write either journals or letters. Some information may be the same for both.

	Advantages	Disadvantages
Journal writing		
Letter writing		

☞ **B Responding to journals** Pages 130–132

Read the following student journal entries from students at a language school outside their own countries. What comment would you write in answer to them, and what, if anything, would you do in response to what is being said?

Journal 1

I am sometimes very lonely because in my house always are lots of people at home. When classes finish I go to my accomodations and study because I have no other thing to do. I want to have many friends but is not easy in this school. At home my best friend and I talk all the time and we go to my house or her house. Here I do not have a best friend.

Journal 2

I need to practice how to reading better because in class is very difficult for me and sometimes you (the teacher) do not let us work with the reading texts in the textbook for long time. We want to be explained every word but you say we must understand general meaning. This is uncomfortable but I should say I like your classes very much.

Journal 3

I want to understand better how to use the big dictionary I have brought. Sometimes is very difficult for me using all the details in it which are very long and many. That is why I rather prefer my electronic dictionary which is in my pocket and not big like the one teachers recommended.

Journal 4

I like my lessons very much, only that I wish that you will correct us more often because I am not knowing sometimes when I am making a mistake. I need to understand when I make wrong English so I can improve myself, but sometimes you are quiet about the English and we are talking a lot without stopping to correct us.

Journal 5

English is great. I am so pleased that I am here in this school and I like very much this city. I go a lot to the pub and clubs like Toxic and Poo Na Na where are lots of my friends. Sometimes I am not sleeping for many hours so I miss some lessons because of sleeping too late.

Task File Key

Chapter 1

A   The diagrams should show the following sequences:
Process 1 – planning • drafting • editing • final version? • editing • drafting • final version
Process 2 – planning • final version
Process 3 – planning • drafting • editing • final version? • planning • drafting • editing • final version

B   **1** S   **2** S   **3** S   **4** S   **5** W   **6** W
     7 S   **8** S   **9** S   **10** S   **11** W   **12** S

Chapter 2

A   **Extract 1** – this is clearly an 'advertisement' or a 'listing', since it misses out space-consuming language such as (*This is an*) *ensemble piece …* . The topic vocabulary, such as *ensemble piece, written by, directed by,* and *with* (+ *names*), clearly suggests some kind of performing art, and the theatre details confirm this to be a typical theatre listing.

Extract 2 – this is a newspaper headline and is identifiable as such by (a) its brevity, (b) its directness, and (c) the words that have been omitted such as articles and auxiliaries. The register is clearly political – a fact deduced by topic vocabulary such as *PM* (Prime Minister), *union, left-winger,* and the phrase *crown falls to.*

Extract 3 – the first thing that alerts us to this being a 'poem' is the format – short lines written one after the other. Then there's the use of many clauses one after the other, and in particular the metaphorical uses (knocking memory, the whole concept of memory being eaten, sitting on the table, being *thump-ripe*).

Extract 4 – the topic and the language both announce this extract as either a 'letter' or a 'postcard'. Throughout, the register is politely informal (*Thank you so much, I hope you had a good time, lots of cute Andalucian towns, Glad to be going back*). The real genre clincher of course is the ending (*Lots of love*).

Extract 5 – this short extract starts as a 'report' since it uses the passive and gives exact details. But the exactness of the details (the age of the people who discovered the bodies, and the throw-away comment about the boy which ends the sentence) show that this is clearly not written in an official register. There is, already, too much opinion in it. The extract, in fact, is the first sentence of a crime novel.

Extract 6 – unlike in the previous extract, there is no overt opinion or comment being made here, but rather an objective description is being attempted. Clearly the register is medical, as shown by the topic vocabulary, yet not written for a scientific journal since the extract lacks some of the markers of that kind of scientific discourse. It comes from a popular medical encyclopaedia.

Extract 7 – whilst the topic is clearly 'cars' (and 'braking'), the mode of address (*Your vehicle is now in a critical situation, keep the brake* *pedal fully depressed*) identifies this extract as coming from some kind of 'manual'. It uses a kind of descriptive imperative (*the ABS allows you to keep control, and reminds you to*) as well as strong imperatives themselves (*Do not reduce pressure*).

Extract 8 – once again, the direct address to the reader (*if you want to dance, you'd be better*) show this to be written in a 'manual' kind of genre, and the extract's use as reference is clearly signalled by (*for more on these, see the box on page 140*). The topic then tells us that we are reading a 'guidebook' about tango in Buenos Aires.

Chapter 3

A **Exercise 1** is a 'writing-for-writing' activity.
Exercise 2 is a 'writing-for-writing' activity.
Exercise 3 is a 'writing-for-learning' activity.
Exercise 4 is a 'writing-for-writing' activity.
Exercise 5 is a 'writing-for-learning' activity.

B 1 EFL   2 ESL   3 ESL   4 EFL   5 EFL
6 ESP   7 EFL   8 ESP   9 ESP

Chapter 4

A **List 1** (*c* pronounced /k/) – cake, call, came, cat, catch, coffee, coin, cost, could, cry, cup, custom
List 2 (*c* pronounced /s/) – cell, cent, certain, cinema, city, cycle, dance, decide, place, policy
When *c* is followed by *e, i*, or *y*, it is pronounced /s/. In all other cases it is pronounced /k/.

B **Suggested answer** – divide the text into segments and give a segment to each group with no punctuation. They have to put in punctuation and then compare it with the original. Alternatively you can give students different bits of the passage both with and without punctuation included. When another group has finished putting in punctuation they can give their work to a group who has the original segment – who can then compare their colleagues' work with the original and make any necessary corrections.

C Open exercise

Chapter 5

A 1 d   2 h   3 c   4 i   5 a
6 g   7 b   8 f   9 e

B Open exercise

C Open exercise

Chapter 6

A This text would be appropriate for students who have reached an upper intermediate level of English. You can ask students what genre this text represents (a 'film review') and what register it is written in (it uses a lot of 'film' topic vocabulary but is at a quite formal and forensic level – which suggests a quality newspaper or journal). You can then get students to investigate the text construction within the genre, using questions such as these: 'What information is given about the film? How does the writer tell us what the film is about? How does he give his opinion? What does he tell us about directors, actors, etc. (and how does he do this)? What grammar and vocabulary is used to perform all of the above purposes?'

When students have been through the review (and others which are similar), they can make lists of words and phrases they want to use. They then all watch the same video of a film, discuss it so that they are sure about facts, actors, etc., and finally write their reviews, constructing them in the same way as the examples they have been looking at.

B 1 Briefing/choice
2 Idea/language generation
3 Data gathering
4 Planning
5 Drafting and editing
6 Final version

Chapter 7

A 1 Responding
2 Responding
3 Correcting
4 Correcting
5 Responding
6 Correcting
7 Responding
8 Correcting
9 Correcting
10 Responding
11 Correcting
12 Responding

B Open exercise

Chapter 8

A Open exercise

B Open exercise
Example answer (possible response for Journal 1) – I am sorry you are lonely sometimes. It is difficult to be in a new country. It might be a good idea if you spend some time in the study centre (more fun than at home?). You can go to some of the student events which you can find on the school noticeboard. You'll make new friends there, I am sure.

(By the way, I would write two or three things a bit differently. I would say *there are always a lot of people at home and it is not always easy …* – and *accommodation* is always singular.)

Punctuation table

Mark	Name and description	Examples
?	**question mark** – signals that a question is asked	*What's your name?* *You're Malaysian?*
!	**exclamation mark** – signals surprise, amazement, or strong emotion	*That's fantastic!*
.	**full stop** (American English: **period**) – marks boundaries between two thoughts/ideas	*He stopped. She stopped too.*
,	**comma** – separates clauses and marks a 'breathing space' between ideas	*He called her name again, and again, and again.*
:	**colon** – signals that something like a list, extra information, or a name is on the way	*There are many kinds of guitar: accoustic, electric, Spanish, or bass guitar.*
;	**semi-colon** – indicates that the main thrust of a sentence continues, but is temporarily halted	*That's the way I see it; it'll go on and on.*
-	**hyphen** – joins two or more words together in a user-friendly way. It is used in:	
1	two-word adjectives where the second part ends in *-ed* or *-ing*.	*the **blue-eyed** girl; the **sad-looking** man; he was **well-informed***
2	two-word adjectives which describe a connection 'between' the two elements.	*the **Paris-Dacca** rally; **Anglo-Argentinean** relations*
3	multi-word adjectives.	*an **out-of-work** actor; a **pay-per-view** channel*
4	nouns, verbs, and adjectives (sometimes) to separate prefixes from word roots.	*a TV **co-production**; her **ex-husband**; he tried to **pre-empt** the attack*
5	in certain words that conventionally have a hyphen. (If in doubt, look in a dictionary.)	*she's **map-reading**; her **make-up***
' ' " "	**inverted commas** (American English: **quotation marks**) – enclose quotations of direct speech. Other pronunciation marks that are part of the direct speech come before the close of the inverted commas. Some people use double inverted commas ("), and some single ('). Having the two allows writers to use quotes within a quote.	*'He said "Watch out!" and I jumped back, which probably saved my life,' Dugie said.*
( )	**brackets** – enclose extra information that is not absolutely necessary and which may seem outside the main thrust of the sentence	*The Cambridge Folk Festival (held in the grounds of Cherry Hinton Hall) is one of the most enjoyable dates in the Cambridge calendar.*
—	**dash** – separates an idea from the rest of the sentence, in a similar way to brackets	*Dashes are used – instead of brackets, sometimes – to separate an idea from the main part of a sentence.*
'	**apostrophe** –	
1	signals a contracted form of a verb	*It's late. They've gone.*
2	indicates possession – note its use after *s* and *x* where *s* is not often used	*Hester's cat; David's dog; Charles' friend; Alex's TV*
A, B	**capital letters** – used for:	
1	proper names	*Jessy, Warwick, Coventry*
2	the first person pronoun	*I agree.*
3	the beginning of sentences	*It is winter. The snow is falling silently.*
4	important roles	*The **President** arrives at six.*

Chapter notes and further reading

Among the many books and articles about writing which have informed the development of this book, a number of titles, past and present, stand out. They have provided endless stimulation, provoked thought and reflection, and informed my own investigation into writing for students of English.

These books are:
Byrne, D (1988) *Teaching Writing Skills*, Longman
Grabe, W & Kaplan, R (1996) *Theory and Practice of Writing*, in 'Longman Applied Linguistics & Language Study' series, Longman
Hedge, T (1988) *Writing*, Oxford University Press
Hedge, T (2000) 'Writing' (Chapter 9) in *Teaching and Learning in the Language Classroom*, Oxford University Press
Hess, N (2001) 'Dealing with written work' (Chapter 4) in *Teaching Large Multilevel Classes*, Cambridge University Press
Hyland, K (2001) *Teaching and Researching Writing*, in 'Applied Linguistics in Action' series, Longman
Tribble, C (1997) *Writing* in 'Language Teaching: a Scheme for Teacher Education' series, Oxford University Press
White, R & Arndt, V (1991) *Process Writing*, Longman

However, while drawing heavily on these sources, my own take on how to teach writing is, of course, my own! Readers who want to follow up these references (and those which are listed by chapter) will be able to see where I have followed the writers' advice, where I have amended it, or where, occasionally, I have not agreed with it.

I would also recommend the following recently published collection of articles researching and discussing second language writing, especially at university level in the USA: Kroll, B (ed.) (2003) *Exploring the Dynamics of Second Language Writing*, Cambridge University Press.

The following references and notes are arranged by chapter. The relevant page number of the chapter is shown on the left. In cases where the book referred to is listed above, only the author and date is given.

Chapter 1
2   *Sir Gawain and the Green Knight*; Anon; Everyman
3   Quotation from Tribble (1997), page 12
     WLC (World Literacy Canada) can be found at http://www.worldlit.ca/
4   **How people write:** see Grabe & Kaplan (1996), Chapters 4 and 5; Hedge (2000), pages 302–316; Tribble (1997), Chapter 5; White & Arndt (1991)
9   **Writing and speaking:** see Byrne (1988), Chapter 1; Hyland (2001), pages 49–53; Tribble (1997), Chapter 3. See also Biber et al. (1999) *Longman Grammar of Spoken and Written English*, Longman
10   **Signs & symbols:** on Internet and text message language, see Crystal, D (2001) *Language and the Internet*, Cambridge University Press

Chapter 2

15 **Different purposes, different writing:** see references in Grabe & Kaplan (1996); Hyland (2001), pages 61–69; Tribble (1997), Chapter 6; Hedge (2000), pages 319–329

19 'it may not always be so' from *The Complete Poems 1904–1962*; Cummings, E.E.; Liveright

23 **Cohesion:** see references in Byrne (1988); Grabe & Kaplan (1996). See also Thornbury, S (1997) *About Language*, Cambridge University Press, pages 120–125

24 **Coherence:** see references in Byrne (1988); Grabe & Kaplan (1996); Tribble (1997), pages 30–33. See also references in Thornbury, S (1997) *About Language*, Cambridge University Press, pages 126, 140

25 Extract from Mahler's *9th Symphony* [Haitink Concertgebouw, Amsterdam], Philips records (464714-2)

Register: see references in Hyland (2001)

27 **Implications for learning and teaching:** on what teachers think about genre see Kay, H & Dudley-Evans, T (1998) 'Genre: what teachers think', *ELT Journal* 52/4

Chapter 3

35 *Just Right: intermediate*; Harmer, J; Marshall Cavendish (2004)

38 *New Headway Intermediate*; Soars, J & L; Oxford University Press (1996)

40 **Creative writing:** quotation from White & Arndt (1991), page 5

Chapter 4

44 **The handwriting challenge:** see Byrne (1988), Chapter 12

45 *Learn English Handwriting*; Hartley, B & Viney, P; Nelson (1987)

47 **Extensive reading:** see Day, R & Bamford, J (1998) *Extensive Reading in the Second Language Classroom*, Cambridge University Press

Teaching spelling: see Shemesh, R & Waller, S (2000) *Teaching English Spelling*, Cambridge University Press

Sounds and spelling: see Kenworthy, J (1987) *Teaching English Pronunciation*, Longman, Chapter 5; Kelly, G (2000) *How to Teach Pronunciation*, Longman, Chapter 8, and Appendix A

50 Extract from *English File: Upper Intermediate*; Oxenden, C & Latham-Koenig, C; Oxford University Press (2001)

51 Extract from *Double Cross*; Prowse, P; Cambridge University Press (1999)

53 **Copying:** Graeme Porte describes his work at the University of Granada in Porte, G (1995) 'Writing wrongs: copying as a strategy for underachieving EFL writers' in *ELT Journal* 49/2

58 Extract from *Opportunities Intermediate*; Harris, M, Mower, D & Sikorzyńska, A; Pearson Education (2000)

59 Extract from *Snapshot Elementary Students' Book*; Abbs, B, Freebairn, I & Barker, C; Pearson Education (1998)

Chapter 5

62 **Engaging tasks:** on the role of engagement in teaching and learning, see Harmer, J (1998) *How to Teach English*, Longman, Chapter 4

Visual, auditory, kinaesthetic: (together with 'olfactory' and 'gustatory' often given the acronym VAKOG) see, for example, Revell, J & Norman, S (1997) *In Your Hands*, Saffire Press

64 **Weather forecast:** this was suggested in conversation by Mario Rinvolucri

65 **Using music:** many of these ideas are adapted from Cranmer, D & Laroy, C (1992) *Musical Openings*, Longman. See also Murphy, T (1992) *Music and Song*, Oxford University Press

69 **Writing poems:** see Holmes, V & Moulton, M (2001) *Writing Simple Poems*, Cambridge University Press

71 'Philip' is from *Poets Live in Cambridge*; ed by Cook, H & Bradbury, Y; Cambridge City Council, Cambridgeshire Libraries and Information Centre, Eastern Arts Association

72 'In two minds' is from *Everyday Eclipses*; McGough, R; Penguin Viking, page 31 (2002)

74 **Dictogloss:** see Thornbury, S (1999) *How to Teach Grammar*, Longman, pages 82–85; Muray, S (2001) 'Dictogloss expanded: how and why to use it' in *Modern English Teacher* 10/3

76 **Writing in groups and pairs (including collaborative writing):** see Hess (2001), Chapter 5. See also Harmer, J (2001) *The Practice of English Language Teaching*, third edition, Longman, pages 114–118

81 **Pen pals, e-mails, live chat:** on penpals and 'key pals' see Hennigan, H (1999) 'Penpals to keypals' in *Modern English Teacher* 8/2; Teeler, D (with Gray, P) (2000) *How to Use the Internet in ELT*, Longman, pages 75–76; Linder, D (2000) 'Making e-mail exchanges really work' in *Modern English Teacher* 9/3

82 John Hughes' form can be found in Hughes, J (2001) 'RU Tchng eEnglish 2?' in *English Teaching Professional* 20

83 The students chatting are quoted in Hyland, K (2001), pages 76–77

Chapter 6

87 **Generating ideas:** see Hedge (1988), Chapter 4 (**pyramid planning** is described on page 154)

88 The poems are from *Haiku ed altre poesie*; ed by Acanfora, F A; Pedrini-editore, Instituto Profesionale Regionale, Aosta (1987)

89 The spidergram is from *Just Listening and Speaking*; Harmer, J; Marshall Cavendish (2004)

100 Linda Pearce's description of her work can be found in Pearce, L (1998) 'Introducing the narrative essay: a painless way to start an academic writing programme' in *Modern English Teacher* 7/1

102 The leaflet is from *Just Right: upper intermediate*; Harmer, J and Lethaby, C; Marshall Cavendish (2004)

103 **Project work:** the 'wheelchair users' guide' was described in Fried-Booth, D (1982) 'Project Work with Advanced Classes' in *ELT Journal* 36/2. See also Fried-Booth, D (2002) *Project Work*, second edition, Oxford University Press. David A Hill describes projects for young learners in Hill, D (1999) 'Projects' in *English Teaching Professional*, 13

104 **Writing for exams:** see Burgess, S & Head K (forthcoming) *How to Teach for Exams*, Longman, Chapter 4

Chapter 7

108 **Responding and correcting:** see Tribble (1997), Chapter 11. See also Muncie, J (2000) 'Using written teacher feedback in EFL composition classes' in *ELT Journal* 54/1

109 **Roles of the teacher:** see Tribble (1997), pages 119–124

111 **Correction symbols:** see Byrne (1988), Chapter 10

113 **No thanks:** the idea of having students say whether they want to be corrected or not comes from Rinvolucri, M (1998) 'Mistakes: 2' in *Modern English Teacher* 7/4

116 Victoria Chan's newspaper project is described in Chan, V (2001) 'The Newspaper Project' in *Modern English Teacher* 10/1

120 'Check and check again' is from *Longman Dictionary of Contemporary English 4, Teacher's Resource Pack*; Harmer, J; Pearson Education (2003)

121 'Marking compositions' is from Hedge, T (1988), page 154

123 **Appropriate homework tasks:** see Painter, L (1999) 'Homework' in *English Teaching Professional* 10

Chapter 8

125 Various uses of letters (see especially Chapter 3) are given in Burbidge, N, Gray, P, Levy, S, Maley, A & Rinvolucri, M (1996) *Letters*, Oxford University Press

127 For the account of diary keeping at NTUS, Singapore, see Krishnan, L & Hwee Hoon, L (2002) 'Diaries: listening to "voices" from the multicultural classroom' in *ELT Journal* 56/3. Examples of diaries and journals are given in Bailey, K & Nunan, D (1996) *Voices from the Language Classroom*, Section 3, Cambridge University Press.

128 On diary writing see also 'Diaries: listening to "voices" from the multicultural classroom'; *ELT Journal* 56/3 (2002); Hook, K & H (eds); Oxford University Press

129 **What kind of journal/notebook?** This is discussed in Kwamlah Johnson, A (2002) 'Journal writing for an audience' in *Modern English Teacher* 11/2

131 The Thailand article can be found in Watson Todd, R, Mills, N, Paolard, C, & Khamcharoen (2001) 'Giving feedback on journals' in *ELT Journal* 55/4

133 **Teacher journals:** see Appel, J (1995) *Diary of a Language Teacher*, Macmillan. Many teachers have kept diaries of themselves as learners of other languages – and used them to draw conclusions about teaching methodology and learning; see, for example, Ahrens, P (1993) 'Diary of a language learner/teacher' in *New Modern English Teacher* 2/2; Gower, R (1999) 'Doing as we would be done by' in *Modern English Teacher* 8/4; McDonough, J (2002) 'The teacher as language learner' in *ELT Journal* 56/4; Shin, S (2003) 'The reflective L2 writing teacher' in *ELT Journal* 57/1

Index